Mystical Roots & Timeless Traditions

Discover the Hidden History of Mysticism Across
Civilizations and Learn How It Still Shapes
Consciousness Today

George Munson

GL Digital Publishing LLC

To my favorite daughter, Nora. Thank you for your continual support and inspiration.

Contents

Introduction

Years ago, during a walk in the woods, I encountered an unexpected moment of stillness. The world seemed to pause, enveloping me in a profound sense of peace and connection. That experience, brief as it was, touched something deep within me, a whisper of something timeless and mysterious. For a moment, everything felt perfectly in place. This was my first brush with mysticism when I realized that the extraordinary could be found in the ordinary.

In this book, mysticism is not an exclusive club but a welcoming space for everyone. It's about those moments when you sense a more profound truth lurking beneath the surface of everyday life. It's about cultivating a connection with the divine, the universe, or whatever you call it. It's not about escaping reality but enhancing it. Mysticism isn't reserved for monks on mountaintops. It's for you and me, here and now, as we navigate the complexities of modern life. You are an integral part of this journey.

This book aims to bring that timeless wisdom into your everyday world. We will explore mystical traditions from around the globe to uncover practices that can help you find clarity and harmony. By integrating these insights, you can transform your daily life into a journey towards inner peace.

My vision for this book is twofold: Firstly, to provide a solid foundation on the history of mystical traditions, giving you a comprehensive understanding of their origins and evolution. Secondly, to offer practical advice for applying these concepts today, equipping you with the tools to incorporate mysticism into your daily life. I want to broaden your understanding and appreciation of these traditions, showing you that they're not relics of the past but living, breathing paths to transformation.

Throughout this book, we'll explore key themes such as the evolution of mysticism, exercises for mystical practice, and the coexistence of science and mysticism. We'll explore various traditions, from Sufi mystics to Zen monks, to challenge your thinking and deepen your reflection.

This book is for individuals like you who seek a deeper spiritual understanding and personal transformation within the context of modern life. Whether you're a spiritual seeker or an intellectual explorer, you'll find something valuable here. This book serves both as an introduction and a deepening of your understanding, offering insights and practices that can be applied to your daily life.

My motivation springs from a passion for helping you break free from conventional thinking and appreciate the richness of mystical traditions. I aim to provide you with clear, reputable guidance filled with vivid descriptions and explorations of mystical experiences.

What sets this book apart is its blend of history with practical guidance. You'll find exercises to incorporate into daily life, making mysticism not just a concept but a valuable tool for personal growth. These exercises are designed to be practical and easily integrated into your routine, empowering you to take control of your spiritual journey. I've avoided jargon, providing a glossary for the few necessary technical terms.

The book is structured to take you on a journey through history, philosophy, and practice. Each chapter builds on the last, integrating scientific perspectives to offer a holistic view of mysticism.

In today's fast-paced world, there is a growing interest in mysticism. Mysticism addresses existential challenges and serves as a path to personal growth and well-being. You can find balance and peace by incorporating mystical practices into your routine.

As you navigate these pages, you can expect to find practical exercises, historical context, and thought-provoking insights. This journey is designed to inform, inspire, and guide you on your mystical path, providing a clear roadmap for your transformation. You are not alone on this journey. This book is here to guide and support you.

I invite you to embark on this journey with an open mind. Explore new perspectives and engage with the material. Apply the insights and practices to your life. Let this book serve as a guide to transformative growth as you uncover the mysticism that lies within.

Chapter One

The Historical Tapestry of Mysticism

Have you ever pondered the awe-inspiring nature of early mysticism? Ancient cultures, long before the invention of telescopes, looked up at the stars with a sense of both awe and understanding. They saw stories, gods, and a cosmos teeming with meaning. This wasn't just stargazing; it was the creation of a tapestry of mysticism, a universal quest for deeper understanding and connection. These moments of connection, where the mundane meets the divine, and the everyday becomes extraordinary, are what we'll explore in this chapter. Join us on a journey back to those early civilizations where mysticism wasn't just a belief system but a way of life.

Mysticism in Early Civilizations Has Ancient Roots

In ancient Egypt, mysticism was as integral as the Nile. The Book of the Dead guided the soul's journey in the afterlife. At the same time, temples like Luxor stood as majestic testaments to the divine's presence on earth. These structures weren't just architectural feats; they were spiritual gateways. Priests practiced rituals connecting them to the gods, seeking wisdom beyond the mortal realm. Meanwhile, in Mesopotamia, the Epic of Gilgamesh not only told a hero's tale but also delved into existential questions about life and death. Ziggurats, towering above the flat landscape, acted as spiritual hubs where people reached for the heavens, hoping for divine favor.

Across continents, indigenous tribes practiced shamanic rituals that were deeply mystical at their core. Shamans acted as bridges between worlds, using trance and dance to communicate with spirits. They didn't just heal bodies; they healed souls, aligning them with the natural rhythms of life. These practices underscore how early societies used mysticism to explain the cosmos and human existence, seeking harmony between the two.

The Hellenistic period witnessed the emergence of Neoplatonism, which infused Greek thought with mystical elements, suggesting that reality was more complex than what met the eye. In the Middle Ages, Christian mysticism flourished with figures such as Meister Eckhart and Hildegard of Bingen, who sought divine union through contemplative practices. During the Islamic Golden Age, a period of cultural, economic, and scientific flourishing in Islamic history, Sufism emerged as a mystical path within Islam, emphasizing love and devotion. These eras shaped mystical practices worldwide, each contributing unique perspectives to our understanding of spirituality.

Mythology and religion played pivotal roles in the development of early mysticism. The Greek mysteries, such as Eleusinian and Orphic rites, were steeped in allegory and symbolic acts that promised to initiate profound transformation. In India, the Vedic traditions explored mystical states through Soma rituals, which involved the consumption of a psychoactive plant to induce a trance-like state, and the hymns of the Rigveda. These ancient texts were chanted during religious rituals. These narratives are intertwined with supernatural experiences, offering pathways to more profound truths.

Nature and the cosmos were not mere backdrops but active participants in mystical thought. Stonehenge stood as a celestial calendar, while Mayan astronomers observed planetary movements with a precision that rivaled modern techniques. For these early mystics, nature was alive with divine presence, its cycles reflecting cosmic order.

Mysticism often merged with religion and philosophy. Theosophy, a complex philosophical system that explores divine wisdom through intellectual inquiry, was one such merger. In Reformation Europe, mysticism challenged dogma by emphasizing personal experience over institutional authority. Spiritual practices, such as offerings and sacrifices, were not empty gestures but acts of devotion that shaped mystical thought, binding communities in shared sacred acts.

Mystical Movements of the Middle Ages

The Middle Ages, often regarded as a time of darkness, surprisingly gave birth to some of the most luminous mystical thinkers. In Christian mysticism, figures like St. John of the Cross emerged, offering profound insights into the spiritual path. His work, "Dark Night of the Soul," speaks to the transformative nature of spiritual trials. It's not about despair, but about growth, much like pruning a plant to encourage fuller blooms. During these times, Hildegard of Bingen also stood out as a woman whose visions and writings were revolutionary. Her mystical experiences were vivid tapestries woven with divine threads, capturing her communion with the spirit. She articulated these experiences through music and writings that inspire seekers today, reminding us of the transformative power of mysticism.

Islamic mysticism, embodied in Sufism, also blossomed during this period. Sufis embraced a path of love and devotion, seeking union with the divine through the heart. With his "Masnavi," the renowned poet Rumi offered verses that transcend time, exploring love as both a human experience and a divine connection. His words remind us that love isn't merely an emotion; it's a pathway to the divine essence within us. Ibn Arabi, another luminary, introduced the concept of Wahdat al-Wujud, or Unity of Being. He posited that all existence is interconnected, a single tapestry woven by the divine hand. This philosophy fostered a worldview where every leaf and stone revealed a more profound truth.

Historical figures such as Meister Eckhart made profound contributions to mystical thought. His sermons and writings offered philosophical insights that challenged conventional views, emphasizing personal experience over dogma. This emphasis on personal experience in understanding mysticism provides a visceral understanding of its transformative power, validating the audience's spiritual journey. Hildegard's visionary experiences complemented such philosophical musings, providing a visceral knowledge of mysticism's transformative power.

Jewish mysticism flourished in this era, with Kabbalistic thought emerging as a profound spiritual tradition. The Zohar, a mystical commentary on the Torah, offered interpretations that unlocked deeper meanings within sacred texts. It invited believers to see beyond the literal to explore the layers of divine wisdom embedded in their faith.

Medieval philosophy wasn't immune to the allure of mysticism. Scholasticism, with thinkers like Thomas Aquinas, sought to reconcile faith with reason. Mystical experiences informed these debates, lending depth to philosophical inquiries that grappled with God's nature and existence.

For those interested in further exploring these mystical traditions, consider reflecting on how these historical insights resonate with your spiritual journey. Reflect on how these historical insights resonate with your path today:

Explore Your Personal Connection to Mystical Texts

- **What mystical text or figure resonates with you most?** Take time to read a passage or write down your thoughts on why it speaks to you.

- **How can you apply these insights to your daily life?** Consider incorporating a practice inspired by one of these traditions into your routine.

These movements remind us that mysticism isn't confined to any single culture or era. It's a universal quest for deeper understanding and connection that transcends time and place. It continues to inspire and guide us in our own lives, forming a spiritual community that spans the globe and the ages.

Pathways of Zen, Tao, and Tantra in Eastern Mysticism

Zen Buddhism offers a unique blend of meditation and philosophy, focusing on direct experience over theoretical understanding. In Zen, the mind is both a tool and an obstacle. Practitioners use koans, paradoxical riddles, or statements designed to break the chains of rational thought. These koans serve as catalysts, pushing the mind beyond its limits into an intuitive state where enlightenment can occur. Imagine pondering a question like, "What is the sound of one hand clapping?" It's not meant to be answered in words but to trigger a deeper awareness. Then there's zazen, or sitting meditation, the heart of Zen practice. It seems simple—just sitting—but it requires intense discipline. Through zazen, practitioners aim to achieve satori, a sudden awakening to the true nature of all things.

Taoist mysticism, on the other hand, flows like a gentle stream, emphasizing harmony with the Tao, the ultimate reality or way. It teaches that the Tao cannot be fully grasped through words or intellect alone. The teachings of Laozi in the Tao Te Ching guide followers toward living according to Tao principles. One key concept is wu wei, or effortless action. It's about aligning oneself so naturally with the flow of life that actions occur without force or struggle. Many Taoists find resonance in nature, seeing it as a manifestation of the Tao's wisdom. In practice, this means moving through life with grace, much like water effortlessly shaping a rock through persistence and adaptability.

Tantric traditions offer another fascinating path within Eastern mysticism, characterized by embracing dualities and transformation through the manipulation of energy. Tantra is often misunderstood in the West as purely focused on physical union, but its scope is far broader. At its core lies the concept of Kundalini awakening—arousing the dormant spiritual energy believed to reside at the base of the spine. This energy moves through chakras or energy centers within the body, leading to higher consciousness and enlightenment. Tantric practices include rituals that symbolize and enact the union of opposites—masculine and feminine energies—leading to spiritual alchemy. The goal is not just personal enlightenment but also universal harmony.

These Eastern traditions didn't develop in isolation. They influenced and were influenced by cultural exchanges across Asia, and in regions like China and Japan, Buddhist and Taoist philosophies often merged into a harmonious blend of beliefs and practices. This syncretism allowed for a rich tapestry of spiritual thought that embraced complexity and diversity. Zen Buddhism, for instance, integrated seamlessly with existing Taoist practices, creating a unique spiritual landscape that values contemplation and spontaneity.

To truly appreciate the depth of these traditions, consider engaging directly with their practices. Try sitting in zazen for a few minutes each day or reflecting on a koan that resonates with you. Explore the Tao Te Ching's teachings daily by practicing wu wei in your actions. If drawn to Tantra, consider learning about Kundalini yoga or meditation practices that focus on chakra alignment. By immersing yourself in these experiences, you can find personal insights into how these ancient paths can enrich your life today.

The Renaissance of Mystical Thought in the West

During the vibrant Renaissance period, a wave of rediscovery swept through Europe. Hidden away in dusty corners were ancient texts that, once unearthed, would profoundly influence Western mystical thought. Among these was the Corpus Hermeticum, a collection of philosophical and theological writings attributed to Hermes Trismegistus. These texts presented a vision of the universe where humans played a critical role in the divine play. Hermeticism, emphasizing the interconnectedness of all things and the pursuit of hidden knowledge, captivated thinkers who sought wisdom beyond the teachings of the church. Neoplatonism also experienced a revival, drawing on Plato's original ideas and expanding them into a mystical framework that viewed reality as a series of emanations from a singular, divine source. This perspective bridges the material and spiritual worlds, inviting exploration into previously inaccessible realms.

Renaissance humanists such as Pico della Mirandola and Marsilio Ficino played a key role in integrating mysticism into their philosophical works. Pico's "Oration on the Dignity of Man" celebrated human potential and divinity within each individual, proposing that humans could ascend to angelic heights or fall to animalistic depths based on their choices. His bold ideas challenged established doctrines and encouraged personal exploration of spirituality. Meanwhile, Ficino dedicated himself to translating and interpreting many mystical texts, including those of Plato and other Neoplatonists. Ficino's translations opened up new avenues for understanding the spiritual dimensions of human existence, bridging ancient wisdom with contemporary thought.

Alchemy and the occult also held a significant place in Renaissance mysticism. Far from the cliché of turning lead into gold, alchemy was a spiritual discipline that sought to transform both the soul and physical matter. Paracelsus, a renowned alchemist, believed that understanding the secrets of nature could lead to profound spiritual insights. He saw alchemy as a means to achieve harmony with nature, encouraging individuals to seek knowledge through direct experience rather than relying solely on traditional authorities.

The Protestant Reformation brought about seismic shifts in religious practices, unexpectedly influencing mystical pursuits. Martin Luther's mystical experiences profoundly reshaped the perception of personal faith. He emphasized individual relationships with the divine, viewing faith as a personal journey rather than mere adherence to rituals. This shift resonated with many who found solace in direct communion with God.

During this era, mysticism wasn't just an intellectual exercise but a lived experience that invited practitioners to engage deeply with both inner and outer worlds. The revival of ancient texts and the integration of mysticism into philosophy marked a period where seeking knowledge became an act of spiritual rebellion against rigid structures. This period reminds us that embracing diverse perspectives can unlock new dimensions of understanding and growth.

Defining Mysticism in a Modern Context

In today's fast-paced world, mysticism emerges not as an ancient relic but as a vibrant, living practice with immense potential for personal transformation. At its core, mysticism is a path to spiritual enlightenment through direct, experiential insight. It emphasizes connecting with something greater, whether you call it the universe, the divine, or simply your inner self. Unlike traditional religious dogmas that often rely on intermediaries or prescribed rituals, mysticism invites you to embark on your spiritual journey. It's experiential, focusing on the profound insights from personal encounters with the ineffable. You don't need a temple or a guru; you need an open heart and a willingness to explore the unknown.

Mysticism is experiencing a resurgence today, appealing to those who find conventional religious structures too rigid and restrictive. The rise of secular spirituality reflects a broader quest for meaning in an increasingly interconnected world. As global communication brings diverse cultures closer, accessing and blending spiritual practices becomes easier. This interconnectedness fosters a sense of shared humanity, making mystical experiences more relatable and achievable. In a time when existential challenges feel overwhelming, mysticism offers a refuge—a way to navigate life's uncertainties with grace and insight. It's not about escaping reality, but about engaging with it on a deeper level and finding peace amid chaos.

While it's easy to confuse mysticism with pseudoscience, it's crucial to differentiate between the two. Mystical experiences may not always align with scientific frameworks, but that doesn't diminish their value. They offer profound personal insights and a connection that transcends empirical validation. Mysticism respects scientific inquiry, acknowledging its role in understanding the physical world while embracing the mysteries beyond it. This balance enables a richer exploration of the human experience, where science and spirituality coexist without diminishing the significance of either.

Mysticism's universal nature transcends cultural and religious boundaries, making it accessible to anyone seeking a more profound understanding. Themes of unity, love, and transformation echo across mystical traditions worldwide—from Sufi poets to Zen monks, each offering unique pathways to enlightenment. Despite diverse expressions, these traditions share common threads that weave a tapestry of spiritual wisdom. Whether through meditation, prayer, or contemplation, mystical practices invite us to explore our inner landscapes and discover truths that resonate with our lives.

Imagine sitting quietly in your living room after a long day, closing your eyes, and taking a deep breath. In that moment of stillness, you might feel a subtle shift—a sense of being part of something larger than yourself. This is the essence of mysticism: finding the extraordinary in the ordinary and seeing the divine in everyday life. It's not reserved for saints or sages but available to anyone exploring its depths.

Mysticism calls us to step beyond the familiar and embrace the unknown with curiosity and courage. It challenges us to question what we think we know and invites us to see the world through new eyes. As you explore the pages ahead, remember that mysticism is not about acquiring knowledge but experiencing transformation. It's about connecting with the deepest parts of yourself and finding harmony with the world around you.

Key Figures in Mystical Traditions

When we think about mysticism, imagining it as a vast, abstract concept is easy. Still, the truth is that it's been shaped by real people with extraordinary lives. Take Teresa of Ávila, for example. She wasn't just a nun but a revolutionary in spiritual practice. Living in 16th-century Spain, Teresa embarked on a path of deep contemplation, often experiencing profound visions. Her writings, such as "The Interior Castle," guide readers through various stages of spiritual development, likening the soul to a castle with many rooms. Each room represents a different level of spiritual growth. Her approach was not just intellectual but deeply experiential, encouraging believers to seek direct communion with God through prayer and meditation.

Fast-forward to the early 20th century, and we meet Paramahansa Yogananda, who introduced Eastern mysticism to the Western world.

His autobiography, "Autobiography of a Yogi," has become a spiritual beacon for many in the West, introducing them to concepts such as meditation and yoga. Yogananda's teachings were revolutionary because they emphasized the universality of spiritual truth, transcending the boundaries of religion. He believed in the power of personal experience and taught that everyone could achieve divine realization through disciplined practice. His legacy endures in the thousands who have followed his teachings and continue to practice Kriya Yoga to this day.

John of the Cross, another towering figure in Christian mysticism, gave us the concept of the "Dark Night of the Soul." This wasn't merely a period of suffering but a profound spiritual transformation where one feels distant from God. John described it as necessary for spiritual growth, leading to a deeper union with the divine. His poetry and prose provide solace and guidance for those navigating their spiritual trials.

In Jewish mysticism, Kabbalah has profoundly influenced spiritual thought. The teachings within works like the Zohar have shaped Jewish mystical practices for centuries, offering deep insights into the nature of God and creation. These teachings encourage adherents to look beyond the literal interpretation of texts and seek hidden meanings that reveal divine wisdom.

Sufi poetry, particularly that of Rumi, has had a profound and enduring impact globally, as well as within Islamic mysticism. Rumi's words transcend cultural and religious boundaries, emphasizing love as a universal force connecting all beings. His teachings have found a place in modern mindfulness practices, inspiring people to live with greater awareness and compassion.

These key figures and their teachings have impacted their immediate communities and left an indelible mark on the broader mystical tradition. Their insights resonate today, offering guidance, inspiration, and a connection to those seeking more profound understanding. As we explore these figures' contributions, we can see how their wisdom applies to modern life, encouraging us to look within and embrace our unique spiritual paths.

As you reflect on these remarkable lives and teachings, consider how their insights might illuminate your path. Mysticism isn't confined to history books; it's alive in our daily choices and quest for meaning and connection. This exploration of mystical traditions isn't just academic—it's an invitation to deepen your understanding and live more fully. Whether you find solace in Teresa's contemplative practices or inspiration in Yogananda's teachings, remember that mysticism is about personal discovery and transformation.

Chapter Two

Comparative Mystical Traditions

Understanding the Differences of Mysticism vs. Religion

You're standing on a bustling street corner. To your left, a grand cathedral towers, its spires reaching for the heavens. To your right, a small, unassuming garden whispers of secrets untold. This juxtaposition captures the essence of mysticism and organized religion. While the cathedral represents structured worship, rules, and community, the garden invites you to wander to discover personal revelations amidst nature's embrace. Mysticism thrives on direct, individual experiences that often bypass formal religious structures. It's about connecting with the divine in a way that's as intimate as it is profound, offering a unique spirituality that complements—but often stands apart from—traditional religious practices.

Organized religion, with its doctrines and rituals, provides a framework for communal belief. It has shaped mystical practices by offering symbols and rituals that mystics have adopted, adapted, or even resisted. Think of religious symbols like the cross or the mandala, which have found their way into mystical practices as tools for meditation and contemplation. Yet, mysticism emphasizes the individual's experience with the divine over communal worship. It's about that personal moment of clarity or enlightenment, often unbound by the confines of religious dogma.

While there are areas of overlap, mysticism and organized religion often diverge in their approaches to spirituality. Religions typically rely on structured rituals and teachings, while mysticism prioritizes personal experiences and interpretations. You might find mystics using religious symbols in their practice, but doing so in ways that diverge from traditional meanings and interpretations. This creates a tension between the orthodox elements of religion and the more fluid nature of mystical exploration.

Historically, this divergence has sometimes led to conflict. Mystics have faced persecution for their beliefs and practices, which were seen as heretical or threatening to religious authorities. Figures like Meister Eckhart and Teresa of Ávila encountered resistance from the Church, and their mystical insights were viewed with suspicion. Today, however, there's a growing acceptance and integration of mystical practices within religious frameworks, as many seek a deeper spiritual experience that complements traditional beliefs.

Understanding these distinctions can have practical implications for spiritual seekers today. If you're navigating your spiritual path within or outside traditional religious contexts, recognizing these differences can empower you to find what resonates with your soul. Mysticism provides a means to explore spirituality on your terms, fostering interfaith dialogue and personal growth.

Your Spiritual Path

- **Reflecting on Your Spiritual Journey:** Consider how mysticism and organized religion have influenced your spiritual beliefs and practices.

- **Identify Areas of Overlap and Divergence:** Consider where your practices align with or diverge from traditional religious teachings.

- **Explore Mystical Practices:** Experiment with incorporating mystical practices, such as meditation or visualization, into your routine to deepen your connection to the divine.

Mysticism serves as a bridge between diverse spiritual traditions, offering insights that transcend doctrinal boundaries and unite them. This understanding fosters dialogue between faiths, enriching each with perspectives that highlight shared human experiences and aspirations for transcendence. Whether you find yourself in a cathedral or a garden—or anywhere in between—know that your spiritual journey is yours to define.

Exploring the Parallels Between Sufism and Christian Mysticism

In the world of mysticism, love stands as a guiding star, uniting paths that otherwise appear distinct. In Sufism, love isn't just a feeling—it's a force that propels the seeker toward the divine. Rumi, the celebrated Sufi poet, encapsulates this beautifully in his verses. His poetry often portrays love as a transformative power that can bridge the gap between the human and the divine. Earthly definitions do not bind this kind of love; it's an ecstatic longing for unity with the ultimate source, a dance of souls reaching toward divine embrace.

Similarly, Christian mysticism holds love as a central tenet. Take St. Teresa of Avila, whose seminal work, "The Interior Castle," maps the soul's journey through stages of spiritual growth. For Teresa, love is the key that unlocks each chamber in the castle of the soul, leading to a profound union with God. Her writings explore how love purifies and elevates, guiding believers through trials and revelations to reach divine intimacy.

Both traditions share an emphasis on ascetic practices as paths to spiritual purification. In Sufism, the whirling dervishes embody devotion through dance, a physical act that mirrors the soul's inner journey toward God. This ritual isn't merely about spinning; it's a meditative state where the dancer becomes one with creation, shedding layers of ego to reveal divine truth. Meanwhile, Christian monasticism offers solitude and fasting as disciplines to quiet the mind and open the heart. Monks retreat into silence to strip away distractions, creating space for divine whispers to be heard.

Symbolism and metaphor play influential roles in expressing mystical truths. Sufi literature abounds with rich imagery, like the rose and the nightingale, to convey concepts of divine beauty and longing. These symbols encapsulate complex spiritual insights in simple yet profound ways. In Christian mysticism, visions of light and darkness often illustrate spiritual revelations—light representing divine presence and darkness symbolizing the soul's struggles. These metaphors transcend words, offering glimpses into mystical experiences that defy ordinary language.

Community and mentorship are crucial in nurturing personal growth within both traditions. Sufi orders revolve around the guidance of a Sheikh, who serves as both mentor and spiritual father. The Sheikh's role is to guide disciples on their path, offering wisdom and insight drawn from personal experience. This relationship is built on trust and mutual respect, fostering a sense of belonging within the mystical community.

Similarly, Christian spiritual direction provides mentorship through seasoned guides who offer counsel and support. These mentors help individuals discern their spiritual path, providing insight and encouragement along the way. Spiritual direction emphasizes listening deeply to both God and self, cultivating an awareness that leads to transformation.

Exploring Your Path

- **Consider Your Spiritual Practices:** Reflect on whether you incorporate elements of love or ascetic disciplines in your spiritual journey.

- **Identify Symbols That Resonate With You:** What symbols or metaphors speak to your soul? Consider how they illuminate your path.

- **Seek Community and Guidance:** Explore opportunities for mentorship or community involvement that align with your spiritual beliefs.

In both Sufism and Christian mysticism, these elements intertwine to create rich tapestries of faith and devotion. They invite you to explore your path with an open heart and a curious mind, trusting that love will guide you toward a deeper understanding. Whether through poetry or prayer, dance or stillness, these traditions offer timeless wisdom for those who seek connection with the divine.

Mysticism in Indigenous Cultures or The Forgotten Narratives

In the heart of indigenous cultures, mysticism doesn't just exist; it thrives. It's woven into every aspect of life, with a profound connection to nature and the earth. Imagine standing in a vast forest, feeling the pulse of life in every tree, every leaf. Indigenous mysticism teaches that all things possess a spiritual essence. This perspective, known as animism, recognizes the sacredness of every mountain, river, and forest. These natural elements aren't mere backdrops to human existence; they are vibrant sites of spiritual significance. Mountains serve not just as physical elevations but as bridges to the divine. Rivers symbolize the flow of life and wisdom. At the same time, forests provide shelter to spirits and serve as places of gathering and reflection.

Storytelling plays an integral role in transmitting mystical knowledge across generations. Through oral traditions, mythological tales come alive, offering insights into the universe's mysteries. Picture elders gathered around a fire, sharing stories that weave together the past, present, and future. These oral histories are more than entertainment; they are lessons encoded with wisdom. Vision quests exemplify personal narratives of transformation. Young individuals venture into nature, seeking solitude and insight. They return not just with stories but with newfound clarity and purpose.

Rites of passage and ceremonies mark crucial spiritual transitions within Indigenous communities. Imagine a young person standing on the threshold of adulthood, participating in initiation rites that symbolize their readiness to embrace new responsibilities. These rituals aren't arbitrary; they signify profound changes in identity and consciousness. Healing ceremonies illustrate the community's reliance on plants and chants to restore balance and well-being. Imagine the rhythmic sound of drums pounding in harmony with the heartbeat of the earth, resonating through these ceremonies as healers invoke the spirits for guidance and insight.

Yet, these rich traditions have faced significant challenges due to colonization. External forces have sought to suppress indigenous spiritual practices, leading to a loss of culture and language. However, a growing movement is emerging to preserve these traditions and breathe new life into them. Efforts to revitalize indigenous languages and rituals are underway, with communities reclaiming their heritage and asserting their spiritual identity. Syncretism reflects this blending of indigenous and introduced religious elements, creating unique expressions of spirituality that honor both past and present.

Colonization's impact on Indigenous spirituality extends beyond physical oppression; it represents an assault on identity and autonomy. Yet, resilience abounds in efforts to reclaim what was nearly lost. Indigenous peoples strive to preserve their heritage by teaching younger generations about their ancestral ways. This revitalization isn't just about holding onto the past; it's about forging a future where these traditions continue to thrive.

Nature Connection

- **Reconnect With Nature:** Spend time in a natural setting, whether it's a local park or a remote forest. Reflect on the presence and essence of the natural world around you.

- **Explore Storytelling Traditions:** Learn about an indigenous myth or legend from your area and consider its lessons.

- **Participate in a Local Ceremony:** Attend a cultural event or ceremony that honors indigenous traditions to gain firsthand experience of these traditions.

By engaging with nature and exploring storytelling traditions, you can deepen your understanding of the powerful connection between indigenous mysticism and the earth. These practices offer valuable insights into living harmoniously with our environment and finding meaning within it.

The Kabbalah and Hindu Mysticism: A Quest for Divine Connection

Imagine peering into a book, not just any book, but one that promises a connection to something greater. This is the essence of Kabbalah, a mystical tradition nestled within Judaism. Its roots stretch back to the 12th century, with its thought profoundly shaping Jewish spirituality. At its core, Kabbalah presents a mystical interpretation of the Torah, suggesting that beneath the literal words lies a deeper, more profound truth. This isn't just about reading; it's about experiencing a revelation that reveals the divine architecture of the universe. Central to this mystical framework is the Tree of Life, a symbol that depicts the spiritual ascent from earthly existence towards divine consciousness. Each branch represents a step, a state of being that the seeker must traverse to achieve spiritual enlightenment. Through meditation and contemplation, practitioners engage deeply with these teachings, seeking not only knowledge but transformation.

Kabbalistic thought is rich with concepts that invite reflection and exploration. Consider the Sefirot, which are divine attributes that serve as channels through which the infinite interacts with the finite world. These ten attributes, such as wisdom and understanding, create a map of divine presence, guiding seekers in their quest to comprehend the nature of the sacred. Another concept is Ein Sof, representing the notion of an unfathomable infinite source from which all creation emanates. It challenges seekers to comprehend the incomprehensible, provoking thoughts about existence and our place within it.

When comparing these metaphysical frameworks with Hindu mysticism, intriguing parallels and contrasts emerge. The Kabbalistic Tree of Life shares similarities with the Hindu chakra system. Both depict pathways to spiritual ascent through symbolic representations. However, where the Tree of Life focuses on divine attributes, chakras represent energetic centers within the human body. These centers govern physical and spiritual health, offering paths to enlightenment through balance and alignment.

Meditation and contemplation are essential practices within both traditions, yet they manifest uniquely in each. In Kabbalistic meditation, practitioners employ techniques that direct focus inward to attain spiritual insight. This might involve visualizing divine names or contemplating sacred texts to access higher states of consciousness. In Hinduism, dhyana involves focused meditation where practitioners quiet the mind and concentrate intensely on a single object or mantra. This practice aims to transcend ordinary awareness and achieve union with the divine.

Sacred texts and esoteric knowledge form the backbone of these mystical explorations. For Kabbalists, the Zohar serves as a mystical commentary on the Torah, offering interpretations that illuminate hidden meanings and divine mysteries. It's not just a text; it's a guide for those seeking a more profound understanding. Similarly, in Hinduism, the Upanishads provide philosophical teachings that delve into the nature of reality and consciousness. These texts offer philosophical insights that challenge readers to reflect on life's ultimate truths.

Both traditions hold transformative views on spiritual development, emphasizing enlightenment as the ultimate goal of life. In Kabbalah, the concept of Tikkun Olam represents humanity's role in restoring balance to the world through righteous acts and spiritual growth. It's not just personal transformation; it's about contributing to universal harmony. Hinduism offers moksha as liberation from the cycle of rebirth. This awakening frees individuals from worldly attachments and leads to unity with Brahman, the ultimate reality.

Each path invites seekers to explore life's profound questions through introspection and practice. They offer tools for connecting with the divine and achieving transformation beyond ordinary understanding. Whether through meditation or study, these traditions provide rich tapestries of wisdom for those seeking deeper connections in their spiritual journeys.

Mystical Insights from Buddhism and Shamanism

Think of a world where the boundaries of ordinary perception blur, allowing a vivid tapestry of consciousness to unfold. Both Buddhism and Shamanism tap into this realm through altered states of consciousness, each offering unique pathways to spiritual exploration. Shamans have long mastered techniques to enter trance states, a practice that involves rhythmic drumming and chanting. These tools help them journey into spiritual realms, seeking guidance and healing. For them, the heartbeat of a drum is more than sound; it's a portal to other worlds where spirits offer wisdom.

In Buddhism, practitioners strive for samadhi, a state of deep meditative absorption. It's a practice of stillness where the mind becomes fully absorbed in an object of meditation, such as the breath or a mantra. This absorption leads to profound insights and a sense of unity with all existence. While the methods differ, both traditions acknowledge the profound value of transcending ordinary consciousness to gain spiritual insights.

Rituals and ceremonies also play vital roles in these mystical traditions. Shamanic practices often involve elaborate ceremonies where drumming sets the rhythm for spiritual journeys. These rituals are communal affairs, uniting people through shared experiences and intentions. They provide structure and support, creating a sacred space for transformation. In Buddhism, traditions such as chanting and making offerings serve similar purposes. They focus the mind and cultivate reverence, setting the stage for more profound meditation and spiritual growth.

Both traditions emphasize the interconnectedness of all life, yet they express this concept in unique ways. Shamans see the world as a web of life, where everything is interdependent and alive with spiritual essence. This perspective fosters a deep respect for nature, seeing it as a partner in spiritual exploration. In Buddhism, the teaching of dependent origination illustrates how everything is interconnected through cause and effect. It highlights that nothing exists in isolation, reminding practitioners of their place within the greater whole.

In these spiritual landscapes, shamans and Buddhist monks serve as guides and healers. Shamans play crucial roles within their communities, acting as intermediaries between the physical and spiritual worlds. They offer healing not just for individuals but for entire communities, using their connection to the spirit world to restore balance and harmony. Buddhist monks, on the other hand, are revered as teachers who transmit wisdom through example and instruction. They guide practitioners on their spiritual paths, offering teachings that illuminate the mind and nurture compassion.

These traditions remind us that spirituality is not just an internal pursuit; it's deeply connected to our relationships with others and the world around us. The lessons they offer encourage us to see beyond ourselves, fostering a sense of unity with all beings.

Mystical traditions offer rich insights that transcend cultural boundaries. They invite us to explore altered states, embrace rituals, and recognize our interconnectedness. By doing so, they challenge us to live with greater awareness and compassion. Next, we'll delve into how modern mysticism continues to evolve, integrating ancient wisdom with contemporary insights.

Chapter Three

The Language of Mysticism

Decoding Mystical Symbols and Archetypes

Think of how you feel when walking into a dimly lit room filled with ancient artifacts and paintings, each one whispering secrets of a time long gone. Mystical symbols have that same enigmatic allure. They serve as bridges to the divine, offering spiritual insight in ways that words alone cannot. Take the lotus flower, for example. In many Eastern traditions, it represents purity and enlightenment. Emerging from muddy waters, it blossoms untouched by the dirt around it, symbolizing the soul's journey to rise above worldly struggles to reach spiritual clarity. The spiral, another potent symbol, captures the essence of growth and evolution. It's found in various cultures, from Celtic carvings to Indigenous petroglyphs, representing the cyclical nature of life and the journey inward toward self-discovery.

Symbols are more than mere images; they're tools for spiritual communication. They encapsulate complex ideas in simple forms, allowing for deeper contemplation. Symbols like these have been used for centuries to convey mystical truths that words often fail to express. They serve as visual shorthand for spiritual teachings, inviting us to explore their meanings and integrate them into our own lives.

Archetypes also play a significant role in mystical literature, appearing as recurring figures that embody universal truths and values. One such figure is the Wise Old Sage, an archetype of wisdom and guidance. This character spans cultures, from Merlin in Arthurian legend to the ancient Taoist sages of China. The sage symbolizes knowledge accumulated through experience and offers advice to those on their spiritual path. Another powerful archetype is the Hero, representing the journey of overcoming obstacles and achieving personal growth. The Hero's journey is a common theme in many mystical stories, inspiring us to face our challenges with courage and determination. Then there's the Seeker, embodying the human quest for meaning and understanding. The Seeker's journey is one of exploration, marked by challenges and revelations that lead to profound personal transformation.

These archetypes resonate with us because they reflect our own experiences and aspirations. They offer models for navigating life's complexities and inspire us to pursue our paths with courage and a sense of curiosity. By recognizing these archetypes within ourselves and others, we can gain insights into our spiritual journeys and find comfort in knowing we're not alone. Each of us is on a unique journey, and these symbols and archetypes help us navigate our paths. This recognition of the personal nature of the spiritual journey fosters a sense of understanding and respect, acknowledging the individuality and uniqueness of each person's path.

Metaphors are another essential element in mystical texts, providing a way to convey complex spiritual truths in relatable terms. Light and darkness are common metaphors used to represent knowledge and ignorance. Light symbolizes illumination and understanding, while darkness represents confusion or lack of awareness. Other metaphors used in mystical texts include the journey as a metaphor for life, the mirror as a metaphor for self-reflection, and the tree as a metaphor for growth and interconnectedness. These metaphors help us grasp abstract concepts by linking them to familiar experiences, making mystical teachings more accessible and relatable.

Imagery plays a crucial role in conveying mystical experiences and bringing abstract concepts to life. Vivid imagery can transport us to realms beyond ordinary perception, offering glimpses of divine beauty and insight. Visions of the divine often feature rich symbolism that resonates deeply with the soul, leaving a lasting impact on those who experience them. These images aren't just visual experiences; they're profound insights into the nature of reality and our place within it. They have the power to transform our understanding of spirituality and life itself, inspiring us to seek deeper connections and insights.

Symbol Exploration

- **Choose a Symbol:** Select a mystical symbol that resonates with you—perhaps the lotus or spiral.

- **Reflect on Its Meaning:** Take a few moments to contemplate its significance and how it relates to your spiritual journey.

- **Incorporate into Daily Life:** Consider how you might integrate the lessons of this symbol into your daily practices or mindset.

By exploring symbols, archetypes, metaphors, and imagery, you gain a richer understanding of mystical traditions and their teachings. These elements invite you to engage with the language of mysticism on a deeper level, encouraging personal reflection and insight. As you delve into their meanings, you open yourself to new perspectives that can transform your understanding of spirituality and life itself.

Understanding Enlightenment and Transcendence

Enlightenment is a term that frequently surfaces in conversations, often used without a full appreciation of its depth and breadth. What does enlightenment genuinely entail? In the realm of mysticism, enlightenment embodies awakening to an enhanced perception of reality, much like discovering spectacles that unveil the unnoticed details of existence. In the esteemed tradition of Buddhism, enlightenment is often synonymous with Nirvana, representing liberation from the relentless cycle of suffering known as samsara. Imagine it as emancipating oneself from a boundless treadmill—a metaphor for the repetitive and often painful nature of life, a release that offers more than just personal serenity; it cultivates a profound understanding that fundamentally alters one's interactions with the world around them and the universe at large. Parallel to this, Hinduism offers the concept of Moksha, which signifies release from the perpetual cycle of rebirth and reincarnation. Picture this as finishing a never-ending marathon and finally resting at a peaceful sanctuary. These metaphors aim to make the concept of liberation more relatable and understandable. While both concepts aim for liberation, whether from suffering or endless rebirth, each offers distinct yet deeply insightful paths to achieve such freedom.

Achieving these exalted states of enlightenment and transcendence involves specific practices designed to quiet the mind and expand the heart. Meditation, a pillar in this journey, allows practitioners to discover a sanctuary of peace within themselves amidst the ongoing cacophony of the world outside. The profound solitude experienced in meditation is a deep and peaceful state of mind that allows for introspection and self-discovery. Numerous meditation techniques exist, from the profound solitude of focusing on one's breath to the rhythmic repetition of a mantra, each unveiling a distinct route toward inner serenity and profound insight. Moreover, contemplative prayer holds a sacred space within the realm of Christian mysticism. This practice transcends simple supplication, aiming instead for communion with a higher power, discovering divine presence amid the hallowed silence and stillness. The hallowed silence and stillness of contemplative prayer refer to the deep peace and tranquility that comes from connecting with the divine. These practices demand not only patience and dedication but also a sincere commitment, promising substantial rewards for those courageous enough to explore them thoroughly.

Transcending beyond the boundaries of ordinary experience has the potential to be profoundly transformative. It's an experience that many describe in terms of ego dissolution. In this sensation, the barriers of self-awareness seem to dissolve, leaving a person feeling interconnected with a grander existence. Ego dissolution is the experience of losing the sense of a separate self, leading to a feeling of unity with the universe. This experience, although liberating, can also be quite daunting. When the ego's incessant murmurs quiet down, it offers a fresh vantage point on life, one where priorities may shift significantly. Suddenly, the seemingly monumental concerns may shrink in significance, while simpler, often overlooked moments gain a newfound depth of meaning. Such transformative experiences have the potential to realign one's priorities and deepen the sense of connection not just with other individuals but also with the universe at large.

However, it's crucial to address several prevailing misconceptions surrounding enlightenment. One persistent myth is viewing enlightenment as a definitive end point, like reaching the peak of a climb and resting eternally at the summit. In reality, enlightenment should be seen as opening the door to a plethora of new possibilities. Another false assumption is that once enlightenment is attained, life becomes effortless and devoid of challenges. That is not entirely true, as life's hurdles continue to appear. Yet, they can be approached with enhanced clarity and reduced attachment. Enlightenment is an enduring journey of growth rather than the achievement of an unattainable state of perfection.

There is also a misconception that enlightenment necessitates a life of renunciation or isolation from the world. While some individuals do walk such paths, numerous others discover enlightenment amidst the vibrant fabric of daily life through interpersonal connections, professional endeavors, and community involvement. The essence of enlightenment is not about retreating from reality but rather about engaging with it more profoundly and earnestly.

The quest for enlightenment is seldom a path free from obstacles. It often presents its own unique set of challenges and roadblocks. As one embarks on this path, doubts may arise, and feelings of inadequacy or frustration may surface. Progress occasionally might feel painstakingly slow, leading to impatience or disillusionment. Nonetheless, these obstacles are integral to the process; they offer opportunities for introspection and growth rather than merely acting as hindrances.

For those seeking enlightenment or transcendence, remember that every step, regardless of its size, holds value and significance. It is not solely about reaching the destination but also about embracing the odyssey itself. Cultivating self-compassion and patience can significantly impact the journey, enriching the experience as it unfolds.

As this chapter unfolds further, the intent is to offer insights that resonate with your personal experiences and aspirations. Whether you gravitate toward meditation or contemplative practices, or find affinity in an entirely different path, these reflections may serve as inspiration on your spiritual journey toward understanding and transformation.

Engaging with these profound concepts may elicit questions or emotions within you—embrace these as intrinsic parts of your exploration in the vast and rich landscape of mysticism!

The Anja Chakra/Third Eye and Spiritual Vision

Imagine a world where perception transcends the obvious, offering glimpses into realms of profound understanding. This is the essence of the Third Eye—a symbol of heightened awareness and spiritual insight. In mystical traditions, the Third Eye is often depicted as a gateway to a deeper level of consciousness. It's like having an inner compass guiding you toward truth beyond the superficial. In Hindu and yogic practices, this concept is associated with the Ajna Chakra, situated between the eyebrows. It's considered the seat of intuition and wisdom, a place where mind and spirit converge. Opening this chakra is believed to enhance your ability to perceive the subtler dimensions of reality, offering clarity in a world often shrouded in complexity.

The Ajna Chakra is believed to be connected to the pituitary gland, which regulates various bodily functions and hormones. This connection highlights the interplay between the physical and spiritual aspects of our being. By focusing on this chakra during meditation or yoga practices, individuals can cultivate a sense of inner peace and alignment with their higher selves.

But how do you awaken this mystical eye? One effective way is through visualization techniques. Imagine yourself standing in a serene garden, at peace. Picture a gentle indigo light softly pulsating at the center of your forehead. As you focus on this light, you might feel a sense of warmth or tingling, indicating the activation of your spiritual center. This process isn't just about imagination; it's about tuning into your body's energy and allowing it to flow freely. Another approach is breathwork or Pranayama. Techniques like alternate nostril breathing can help balance your energies, preparing your mind for deeper exploration into your inner world.

The Third Eye is deeply connected to intuition—your ability to understand something instinctively without the need for conscious reasoning. It's that gut feeling you get when something feels right or wrong, even if you can't articulate why. This intuitive insight allows you to recognize signs and symbols that might otherwise go unnoticed. Imagine walking down a busy street and suddenly noticing a feather on the ground. To some, it might seem insignificant, but through the lens of intuition, it could symbolize guidance or reassurance from the universe.

Different cultures have their unique perspectives on this mystical concept. In ancient Egypt, the Eye of Horus holds significant meaning. It's not just an image of protection but also a symbol of insight and clarity. The Egyptians believed this symbol could ward off evil while offering wisdom to those who understood its more profound significance. This connection between sight and insight across cultures highlights a shared human desire to see beyond the ordinary.

To further enhance your understanding of spiritual vision, consider incorporating these practices into your daily life. Set aside time each day for meditation or quiet reflection. Observe how your intuition guides you in decision-making and personal interactions. Please pay attention to recurring symbols in your life and explore their meanings. Keep an open mind as you explore these practices, allowing yourself to be curious and receptive to new insights.

Breathwork techniques such as alternate nostril breathing (Nadi Shodhana) are also effective in balancing and activating the Ajna Chakra. This practice involves inhaling through one nostril while exhaling through the other, creating harmony between mind and body. By incorporating these practices into daily routines, individuals can gradually enhance their spiritual vision and deepen their connection to themselves and the world around them.

As you explore these concepts further in your spiritual journey, remember that awakening your third eye is not about forcing change but rather inviting awareness into your life with openness and curiosity. Embrace each step along this path with patience as you cultivate deeper connections within yourself while expanding your perception outward toward life's mysteries yet to be discovered.

By embracing the concept of the Third Eye, you're opening yourself up to new ways of seeing and understanding the world around you. This isn't just about acquiring knowledge; it's about experiencing transformation on a deeper level. As you continue exploring these practices, remember that spiritual vision is a lifelong journey—one that invites you to look beyond the surface and discover hidden truths within yourself and the universe.

The Symbolism of Kundalini

When we explore the symbolic representation of Kundalini, it becomes clear that this energy is deeply rooted in centuries-old traditions, imbued with a wealth of layers of meaning. The depiction of Kundalini as a coiled serpent varies across cultures. Still, it often serves as a metaphor for the dormant power and potential that lie within each individual. In ancient texts and spiritual practices, the serpent symbolizes wisdom, transformation, and the cyclical nature of life—shedding old skins to renew itself, much like the human spirit evolving through spiritual growth. Kundalini's journey through the chakras is not merely metaphorical; it reflects the potential for profound transformation as one ascends through levels of consciousness, depicted as the chakras, each symbolizing different aspects of existence, from basic survival instincts at the base to the divine consciousness at the crown.

The Journey of Awakening

The process of awakening Kundalini is as personal and unique as it is universal. Experiencing the initial awakening is often likened to being struck by lightning—a sudden, intense unveiling of what was once hidden. Imagine being in a dark room, and suddenly, the lights are turned on; everything is revealed in sharp detail. This initial shock, both exhilarating and bewildering, is followed by subtle shifts in your sense of self. The body may react physically, manifesting as tremors or sensations of warmth spreading upward from the spine. For some, it is an overwhelming sense of euphoria or a marked increase in creativity and insight. These experiences are tangible evidence of the energy moving through you, catalyzing change and growth.

The integration phase can be thought of as building a new foundation upon which your evolving consciousness stands. It involves reconciling the old self with the emergent, encapsulating the essence of reconstruction—an architectural undertaking of your spiritual and emotional being. For some, this may involve adopting new lifestyle practices that support and sustain this heightened awareness, such as refining one's diet, establishing meditation routines, or engaging in reflective journaling. The key lies in crafting a lifestyle that respects this awakened state while ensuring you remain grounded, clear-headed, and compassionate as you navigate day-to-day realities.

Dispelling Myths and Embracing Truths

Despite its mystical allure, the awakening of Kundalini invites a plethora of misconceptions. It is crucial to confront these myths head-on to pave a clear path for those seeking this transformative journey. One prevalent myth is that Kundalini awakening is a rare, near-mythical occurrence only accessible to a select few. However, many teachers and practitioners affirm that, while unique to each individual, it is attainable and can be cultivated through dedicated practice. Another myth suggests that Kundalini, once awakened, results in instant enlightenment, freeing one from life's challenges. In truth, while providing profound insights and a deeper connection to universal truths, it also demands responsibility to process, adapt, and grow through each subsequent revelation.

Practical Steps and The Role of Mentorship

As you embark on this sacred exploration, employing grounding practices becomes indispensable. Walking on the earth, feeling the soil underfoot—these acts tether your consciousness to the present, preventing it from being swept away by an overwhelming tide of energy. In addition to grounding techniques, purposeful breathwork, such as Pranayama, cultivates an inner equilibrium, ensuring a harmonious flow of energy and preventing blockages that might impede your journey.

Navigating this spiritual terrain without guidance can feel like exploring an ancient map without a compass. Esteemed mentors act as guides, illuminating the path with their wisdom and experience. Their presence is vital in addressing fears and clarifying doubts, especially during unpredictable turns your awakening might take. They provide a safe space in which one's spiritual questions are met with empathy and profound understanding. A guiding hand can facilitate breakthroughs, steer you through challenges, and celebrate the milestones along your path to unlocking the full potential of a fully awakened Kundalini.

The Journey Continues

Embarking on a journey toward Kundalini's awakening becomes a poignant reminder that enlightenment is not a distant destination but a continuous unfolding—a journey marked by growth, potential, and self-discovery. Each stage of this process invites you to deepen your connection with your inner self and the world around you, forging bonds between the seen and the unseen, the physical and the spiritual. In the upcoming chapter, we will journey beyond the mystical to explore how embracing spirituality in daily life can lead to balance, harmony, and an enriched existence, seamlessly interwoven into the fabric of one's routine as it guides you toward living a more fulfilling, conscious life.

Chapter Four

Mystical States of Consciousness

Identifying Mystical Experiences

See yourself in a serene forest clearing, the tall trees swaying gently in the breeze. Suddenly, you're enveloped in a profound sense of peace and connection, as if the boundaries between you and nature have dissolved. This is a glimpse of a mystical experience—moments when the ordinary world is infused with deep personal meaning. These experiences are deeply subjective, often characterized by ineffability—the idea that they transcend words—and a noetic quality, meaning they impart a sense of deep personal knowledge or insight. You may feel a sense of unity with all things, as though you're part of a larger, interconnected whole.

It's crucial to distinguish these mystical moments from other altered states, such as dreams or hallucinations. Mystical experiences, with their transformative power, typically involve a reduction in self-referential thinking, where your usual sense of self becomes less pronounced. They often lead to profound and lasting transformation, leaving an indelible mark on your perspective and how you engage with life. They inspire hope and a sense of possibility.

Mystical experiences, while varying widely among individuals, share universal themes. Your cultural background and personal context can shape these experiences, influencing how they're interpreted and integrated into your life. For example, while one person might experience a mystical moment during meditation, another might find it through art or music. This universality of experience connects us all in a larger narrative of human consciousness, making us feel part of a shared journey.

Consider William James's study of religious experiences, which highlighted the diversity and commonality of these transformative events (The Varieties of Religious Experience). Modern accounts from meditation practitioners echo this richness, showcasing how deeply personal yet universally resonant mystical experiences can be.

Exploring Your Mystical Experiences

- **Recall a Moment of Connection:** Think about a time when you felt deeply connected to something greater than yourself. What sensations and emotions did you experience?

- **Reflect on Any Lasting Changes:** How did this moment influence your beliefs, values, or way of living?

The Science of Transcendence

Consider the brain as a complex orchestra, where every neuron plays a part in the symphony of consciousness. When you experience a mystical state, this orchestra conducts a unique performance. Scientists have discovered that during these moments, your prefrontal cortex and temporal lobes become particularly active. These regions are associated with complex thought processes and emotional regulation. Neurotransmitters, such as serotonin, which influence mood and perception, play a crucial role. It's as if your brain releases a cocktail of chemicals that open the doors to transcendental awareness.

Meditation and mindfulness practices offer a practical gateway to these mystical experiences. Regular meditation doesn't just calm your mind; it transforms your brain. Research has shown that consistent practice can lead to changes in brain plasticity, meaning your brain becomes more adaptable and resilient. Studies even suggest an increase in gray matter density, particularly in areas related to memory, empathy, and stress regulation. It's like giving your brain a workout that makes it stronger and more flexible, opening the door to transcendental awareness.

The mysteries of quantum physics add another layer to our understanding of mystical states. Theories about quantum entanglement suggest that particles remain connected across vast distances, hinting at a universe more interconnected than we might imagine. Some theorists propose that consciousness itself may be a quantum phenomenon, potentially explaining the profound unity experienced in mystical states. However, the subjective nature of these states poses a challenge to scientific inquiry. Measuring something as personal as a mystical experience requires an interdisciplinary approach that combines neuroscience, psychology, and philosophy, engaging us in a collaborative effort to unravel these mysteries.

The limitations of scientific methods become apparent in this context. While brain scans reveal patterns, they can't capture the essence of the experience itself. This makes the exploration of mystical consciousness both thrilling and enigmatic. It's essential to acknowledge that the subjective nature of these states presents a challenge to scientific inquiry, and measuring something as personal as a mystical experience necessitates an interdisciplinary approach that combines neuroscience, psychology, and philosophy.

Quantum Mysticism to Bridge Science and Spirit

You're standing at the crossroads of two worlds: the precise realm of quantum physics and the vast, mysterious expanse of mystical philosophy. This intersection is known as quantum mysticism, a concept that attempts to explain non-material phenomena through the lens of quantum mechanics. At its core lies quantum entanglement, the idea that particles, once connected, remain linked across space and time. Mystics have long spoken of interconnectedness, and quantum theories echo this sentiment, suggesting a universe where everything is entangled in a cosmic dance.

Quantum mechanics presents intriguing parallels with mystical teachings. The observer effect, a principle stating that the act of observation can alter the outcome, challenges our understanding of reality. This aligns with mystical views that consciousness shapes our world. Concepts like non-locality and duality further blur the line between science and spirituality, hinting at a reality where separation is an illusion.

However, not everyone embraces quantum mysticism without reservation. Critics argue that some interpretations veer into pseudoscience, misrepresenting quantum physics to support mystical claims. It's crucial to maintain scientific rigor, ensuring that explorations into these realms remain grounded in empirical evidence.

Despite controversies, quantum mysticism offers fertile ground for new theoretical models. Some researchers explore how consciousness might play a role in quantum field theory, potentially bridging gaps between science and spirituality. This interdisciplinary approach could foster collaborations that expand our understanding of both domains.

Bridging Science and Spirit

- **Consider Your Views on Interconnectedness:** Reflect on how the concepts of quantum entanglement and mystical interconnectedness resonate with your beliefs.

- **Explore Scientific and Mystical Parallels:** Identify areas where science and spirituality intersect in your understanding of reality.

Consciousness Studies Give a Scientific Perspective

Consciousness studies are like the frontier of the mind, constantly evolving as researchers strive to comprehend this elusive phenomenon. At its core, consciousness asks how subjective experiences arise from physical brain processes. Integrated Information Theory (IIT) is one of the leading theories, suggesting that consciousness comes from the brain's ability to integrate and process information. Yet, the "Hard Problem of Consciousness," a term coined by philosopher David Chalmers, remains unsolved. It questions how and why we have conscious experiences at all, especially those that feel mystical or transcendent.

Scientists employ various methodologies to explore these altered states of consciousness. Functional magnetic resonance imaging (fMRI) and electroencephalography (EEG) are pivotal tools in this research. They enable scientists to observe brain activity in real time, providing insights into how different areas of the brain are activated during mystical states. Experiments often focus on altered perception and awareness, examining how these experiences change one's worldview and self-understanding.

These findings have profound implications for the study of mysticism. They highlight how attention and intention can shape experiences, providing a scientific basis for practices like meditation. As we learn more about the brain's role in generating these states, we gain a deeper appreciation for the subjective nature of mystical experiences. Philosophical questions naturally arise, challenging our notions of materialism versus dualism. The nature of reality and perception becomes a focal point, pushing us to consider whether our everyday experiences are just the tip of an iceberg of consciousness waiting to be explored.

Psychological Implications of Mystical States

Mystical experiences can be life-changing, leading to profound psychological shifts. You might find a newfound sense of purpose, feeling more connected to the world around you. Many people report a significant reduction in anxiety and depression. It's as if these experiences shine a light into the darker corners of your mind, bringing clarity and a sense of peace. The impact isn't just temporary; it can lead to lasting personal growth and a deeper understanding of yourself and your place in the universe.

These experiences are finding their way into therapeutic settings. Psychedelics, once taboo, are being reconsidered for their potential in therapy. Under controlled conditions, they can induce mystical states that help people break free from negative thought patterns. Mindfulness-based stress reduction techniques also tap into these states, promoting mental well-being. Such practices encourage you to stay present and accept your experiences without judgment, fostering resilience and emotional balance.

Mystical experiences often reshape your identity and worldview. You might experience a dissolution of ego boundaries, where the lines between you and others blur. This shift can enhance your empathy and compassion, making you more attuned to the feelings and needs of those around you. However, integrating these experiences into daily life isn't always easy.

There is a risk of spiritual bypassing, where you may use spiritual insights to avoid confronting personal issues. Changes in your social relationships may also arise as you evolve, leading to challenges in maintaining connections with those who haven't shared similar experiences.

Navigating these changes requires patience and an open mind. It's essential to ground yourself and connect with supportive communities that understand your transformative journey.

Mystical Consciousness and Spiritual Enlightenment

Try to picture a deep, peaceful lake where the surface is perfectly still. Spiritual Enlightenment is like seeing the entire reflection of the sky without a ripple. In the realm of mystical consciousness, Enlightenment is the pinnacle—a realization of non-duality, where you see beyond the illusion of separateness and experience liberation from suffering. It's about understanding that all life is interconnected, dissolving the barriers that often confine us to narrow perceptions.

The pathways to Enlightenment are as diverse as they are profound. The Eightfold Path in Buddhism offers a structured approach, emphasizing correct understanding, intention, speech, action, livelihood, effort, mindfulness, and concentration. These principles aim to cultivate wisdom and ethical conduct, guiding practitioners toward awakening. In contrast, Bhakti yoga focuses on devotion and love for the divine. Through prayer, song, and ritual, practitioners seek a personal connection with a higher power, transcending the ego and embracing unity.

Consider people like Ramana Maharshi, whose teachings and life continue to inspire seekers worldwide. He taught self-inquiry as a means to discover one's true nature. Modern spiritual teachers also share insights from their journeys, each offering a unique perspective on the varied paths to Enlightenment.

The Enlightenment's influence extends beyond individuals to society as a whole. Enlightened leaders often inspire transformative changes, bringing compassion and insight into their communities. Cultural narratives around enlightened beings shape values and social norms, highlighting ideals of wisdom and inner peace. These stories remind us of our potential to rise above challenges and make a positive contribution to the world around us.

The Neuroscience of Mystical Experiences

See your brain as a bustling city, with different regions communicating like neighborhoods through intricate pathways. When you experience a mystical state, something extraordinary happens. Neuroscientists have discovered that the Default Mode Network (DMN), a part of the brain involved in self-referential thought, often quiets down. This deactivation enables a sense of ego-dissolution, where the boundaries of the self blur, paving the way for profound spiritual experiences. Meanwhile, neurotransmitters like serotonin and dopamine, often referred to as the "feel-good" chemicals, flood your brain, enhancing feelings of bliss and connection.

During mystical experiences, your body can undergo physical changes as well. Heart rate often slows, aligning with deep meditative states, while breath patterns shift, becoming more rhythmic and deliberate. These physiological changes are not just side effects; they can deepen the experience and bring about a sense of harmony and balance.

The intersection of neuroscience and spirituality offers exciting possibilities for enhancing mystical practices. By understanding how the brain functions during these states, mindfulness techniques can be tailored to maximize their benefits. Imagine using this knowledge to refine your meditation practice, making it even more effective at fostering inner peace and spiritual growth.

Mysticism in the Age of Technology with Opportunities and Challenges

In today's digital age, technology radically reshapes how we experience and share mystical practices. Virtual reality, for instance, offers a new frontier for simulating mystical experiences. Imagine donning a VR headset and finding yourself in a serene temple or an expansive desert, where every sense is profoundly engaged. It's not just about visuals; it's about crafting an immersive environment where you can explore inner landscapes without leaving your room. Social media also plays a crucial role in connecting spiritual communities worldwide. You can now participate in discussions, share insights, and find like-minded souls with just a few clicks.

But while technology opens doors, it also presents challenges. On one hand, meditation apps make mindfulness more accessible than ever, democratizing access to ancient practices. On the other hand, the digital world teems with distractions that can lead to superficial engagement. The constant ping of notifications may pull you away from deep contemplation, diluting the very essence of these practices.

New platforms, such as online retreats and virtual gatherings, redefine how groups explore mystical states together. Wearable technology tracks physiological responses, providing insights into your body's reactions during meditative states and bridging the gap between subjective experience and measurable data. However, integrating tech into spirituality raises ethical questions. Digital spiritual communities must navigate privacy concerns—after all, your most personal moments could become data points. As artificial intelligence begins to influence even spiritual experiences, we face new philosophical challenges about what it means to have an authentic mystical experience in the digital age.

States of Cosmic Consciousness in Reaching Beyond Ordinary Awareness

Imagine feeling a profound connection to everything around you, as if the universe itself is whispering secrets directly into your soul. This is cosmic consciousness, a heightened state of awareness where you experience unity with the universe. It's like seeing the world through a lens that reveals the interconnectedness of all things. In this state, your perception expands beyond usual sensory limitations, offering a glimpse into a reality that feels both vast and intimate.

There are various pathways to achieving this state. Psychedelic experiences using substances like psilocybin can temporarily dissolve barriers between self and the cosmos, providing insights that feel both profound and transformative. Meanwhile, deep meditative practices cultivate cosmic consciousness through prolonged focus and stillness. By turning inward, you gradually shed layers of ego-centric thought, opening yourself to a broader awareness that transcends individual identity.

Experiencing cosmic consciousness can lead to significant personal transformation. The dissolution of ego allows for a redefinition of self, where identity blends with a collective existence. This shift often enhances empathy and compassion, fostering a deeper connection with others and the world around us. It's as though you're no longer just an individual but part of a greater whole, leading to an enriched perspective on life.

However, integrating these experiences into daily life can be challenging. Returning to everyday routines after touching such expansive awareness requires grounding practices. Techniques such as mindful breathing or connecting with nature help maintain balance and bring insights from cosmic consciousness into your everyday existence. These practices root you in the present, allowing you to carry the wisdom of cosmic awareness into the mundane aspects of life, enriching them with newfound depth and clarity.

The Role of Synchronicity in Mystical Realizations

While walking through life, seemingly random events begin to align with uncanny precision. This is synchronicity, a term coined by Carl Jung to describe meaningful coincidences that defy logical explanation. In mystical traditions, such fortuitous happenings hold great significance. They are seen as glimpses of the universe's hidden order, offering guidance and insight into its workings. Jung's exploration into these phenomena revealed their potential to act as catalysts for spiritual growth, pushing individuals toward deeper understanding and connection with the divine.

Synchronicity often nudges us toward paths we might not have considered otherwise. A chance meeting with a stranger who shares your deepest passions might lead to a life-altering decision. It could be the universe's way of saying, "Trust this direction." Such occurrences frequently guide our major life choices, acting as markers on our spiritual maps. This inner guidance encourages us to trust the signs and messages we receive, even when they feel mysterious or inexplicable.

Interpreting synchronicities requires tuning into a symbolic language unique to each person. What one individual perceives as a mere coincidence might hold profound meaning for another. It's about understanding the personal significance of these symbolic events and recognizing patterns that resonate deeply within your soul. Mystical literature brims with examples of synchronicity leading to profound realizations. Historical and contemporary texts offer case studies where these meaningful coincidences have sparked epiphanies, guiding individuals toward spiritual revelations they never imagined possible. These stories underscore how synchronicity enriches the tapestry of our lives, weaving connections that transcend the ordinary and lead us toward extraordinary insights.

Navigating Skepticism to See if Mystical Experiences are Real

Skepticism isn't just a barrier; it's a tool for growth. When you approach mystical experiences with healthy skepticism, you engage in critical thinking that deepens understanding. It's crucial to distinguish constructive skepticism, which questions and explores, from cynicism, which dismisses and denies. This distinction enables a genuine pursuit of truth.

Scientific and philosophical perspectives offer diverse views on mystical experiences. The debate between dualism, which posits a separation between mind and body, and materialism, which views consciousness as entirely physical, highlights the complexity of understanding these states. Some scientific studies lend support to the reality of mystical experiences, suggesting they are not merely products of imagination.

Skeptics often argue that mystical experiences are hallucinations or the result of the placebo effect, where expectation shapes perception. While these arguments warrant consideration, they don't account for the profound insights and transformations many report after such experiences. Open-minded exploration can lead to personal revelations. Experiential learning in mysticism offers direct understanding, while embracing uncertainty invites growth.

Accepting mystical experiences as real has wide-ranging implications. In healthcare, they could offer new therapeutic approaches, while culturally, they might shift narratives towards a broader acceptance of spirituality. Engaging skeptically doesn't mean shutting down conversations; it means engaging them thoughtfully. It opens doors to dialogue where science and spirituality intersect. Respectful discourse fosters mutual understanding.

Remember that skepticism and belief aren't enemies but partners in exploration. As we move forward, consider how embracing both can enrich your spiritual path and prepare you for the next chapter's insights into practical mystical exercises for daily life.

Chapter Five

Practical Mysticism for Daily Life

Meditation Techniques for Beginners

It's a serene Sunday morning, the sun's rays delicately filtering through your window, heralding a day brimming with endless possibilities. You decide to carve out some precious time for yourself, a sacred pause to breathe, reflect, and gather your thoughts before immersing yourself in the day's bustling activities. Meditation is not merely about sitting in silence; it represents the act of creating a personal oasis amidst life's inevitable chaos. Let's begin with the essence of simplicity. Picture yourself directing your focus on your breath. Each gentle inhale and exhale is like the rhythmic ebb and flow of waves caressing the shore. This breath-focused meditation prioritizes simplicity over complexity, emphasizing accessibility and serenity. Find a tranquil corner in your home, perhaps a snug chair or a spot on the floor adorned with a soft cushion, and allow yourself to be. Gently close your eyes and immerse in the breathing process. Feel the invigorating air as it fills your lungs and then drifts away slowly. This practice serves as an exercise in presence, a chance for thoughts to drift by like floating clouds without the necessity to chase after them.

Another technique to explore is the body scan, a gentle and exploratory sojourn through your internal landscape. Initiate this journey at your toes, mindfully escalating your attention upward. Take a mental note of every sensation, acknowledging areas of accumulated tension and consciously choosing to let go. This exercise is devoid of judgment regarding your discoveries; it is centered on acknowledgment and release. Such an approach helps you ground yourself, cultivate awareness of where stress is manifested in your body, and learn the art of dissipation.

Now, you are far from alone if you find your mind wandering or if restlessness ensues—that is not only a common but a natural part of the process. It's all too easy to become ensnared by the day's forthcoming agenda or the worries that linger from yesterday. We understand that maintaining focus can be a challenge, and that's okay. Setting aside a specific time and establishing a habitual space can be instrumental. Perhaps it's the quiet solitude of the morning or the calm preceding slumber. Crafting a set ritual sends a signal to your brain that this time is your cherished period for tranquility and introspection.

If you find it challenging to maintain focus, don't worry. Guided meditation apps can be invaluable allies. They offer a structured approach and guidance, transforming the journey into a less daunting endeavor. Apps such as Calm or Headspace offer sessions carefully crafted for beginners, easing you into meditation practice with gentle nudges and soothing voices designed to enhance relaxation.

Cultivating a meditation habit is paramount. Initiate the journey with just five minutes a day, a duration manageable and far from overwhelming. Over time, as familiarity and comfort grow, you can naturally extend these sessions. The intent is consistency, not perfection. As with any burgeoning skill, it demands both practice and patience. As you embark on this journey, you'll experience a sense of accomplishment and empowerment that'll motivate you to continue.

Quick Tips for Meditation Success:

- **Create Your Space:** Deliberately allocate a spot that exudes comfort and is devoid of distractions, a haven for your practice.

- **Set a Timer:** Begin with brief intervals of 5-10 minutes, gradually lengthening them as your readiness increases.

- **Try Guided Sessions:** Integrate apps or online resources into your routine for added support and variety, enriching your experience.

Recall that meditation is an intensely personal voyage. There exists no absolute right or wrong method to pursue; it revolves around what resonates with you. The trail to inner peace isn't a sprint; it manifests as a leisurely stroll taken each day, one deliberate, mindful step after another. As practice becomes ingrained, moments of stillness will increasingly seep into your daily life, equipping you to navigate life's challenges with greater ease and grace. You have the freedom to choose the method that best suits you, and we respect that choice.

Mindful Breathing as a Gateway to Presence

By focusing on your breath, you create a bridge between your body and mind, enabling you to experience the present moment with clarity and ease. Breath awareness is the cornerstone of this practice. It involves directing your attention to the natural flow of your breath without trying to change it. As you breathe in and out, notice the rise and fall of your chest or the sensation of air passing through your nostrils. This gentle focus helps anchor your mind, reducing mental chatter and enhancing presence.

Counting breaths is another technique that can help maintain focus. Begin by inhaling deeply and silently counting "one" in your mind. Exhale and count "two." Continue this pattern up to ten, then start again. This cyclical process provides a rhythm to your breathing, keeping your attention from wandering. When your thoughts start drifting, gently bring them back to the count. This practice teaches patience and concentration, essential skills for cultivating mindfulness.

Beyond its meditative benefits, mindful breathing offers significant physiological and psychological advantages. Stress often manifests as elevated cortisol levels, but controlled breathing can help lower these stress hormones, promoting relaxation. It's like giving your nervous system a mini vacation amidst life's chaos. When emotions run high, using breath as a tool to navigate turbulence can restore balance. By taking slow, deep breaths, you can calm your mind and regain control over emotional responses, fostering resilience and stability.

Mindful breathing also sharpens concentration and focus. As you train your mind to return to the breath whenever it wanders, you build mental clarity. Over time, this practice helps improve attention span and cognitive function, making it easier to remain focused on tasks or conversations.

To integrate mindful breathing into daily life, consider starting with box breathing, a straightforward yet effective exercise. Inhale for a count of four, hold for four, exhale for four, and hold again for four. This method encourages even breathing, promoting relaxation and reducing anxiety. For those seeking harmony between body and mind, alternate nostril breathing offers balance by engaging both hemispheres of the brain. Close one nostril with a finger, inhale through the open nostril, switch sides, exhale through the other nostril, and repeat.

In spiritual practices, breath serves as an anchor during meditation, deepening mystical experiences and insights. By focusing on the breath, you create a stable foundation from which to explore higher states of consciousness. This connection between breath and meditation enhances awareness of subtle energies and fosters a deeper connection to the present moment.

Mindful breathing acts as a gateway to presence, offering a path to heightened awareness and emotional regulation. With consistent practice, it evolves from a simple exercise into a powerful tool for navigating life's challenges with greater ease and grace. So take a moment now—close your eyes, breathe deeply, and let yourself drift into the peaceful space of mindful presence.

Visualization Techniques for Spiritual Growth

Close your eyes, not to shut out the world, but to open a window into your mind's eye where possibilities await. Visualization in spiritual practice is similar to painting a canvas with your thoughts, transforming your imagination into a powerful tool for manifesting your spiritual goals and insights. This isn't just daydreaming, it's about crafting vivid mental imagery that shapes your reality. Pretend you're standing in a field under a starry sky, with each star representing a cherished aspiration. With every deep breath, visualize those stars shining brighter, symbolizing your intentions and gaining strength and clarity.

Guided imagery offers a structured approach to visualization, leading you through a mental narrative to explore your inner landscapes. It's like embarking on a journey through a lush forest where each step takes you closer to understanding your desires and fears. This method enables you to engage with your subconscious, unlocking insights that lie beneath the surface. On the other hand, creating a vision board is a powerful practice in its own right. Gather images, words, and symbols that resonate with your spiritual aspirations and arrange them in a way that speaks to you. This tangible representation keeps your intentions front and center, serving as a daily reminder of the path you're on.

Crafting personalized visualizations involves more than just closing your eyes and hoping for the best. It begins with setting clear intentions. Before diving into visualization, take time to clarify what you wish to manifest or understand. Perhaps it's inner peace or the courage to tackle challenges—whatever it's, make it concrete in your mind. Next, incorporate symbolic imagery that holds personal significance for you. If you've always been drawn to the ocean, envision yourself standing by the shore, letting its vastness remind you of life's endless possibilities.

However, visualization isn't without its hurdles. One common challenge is distractions—those pesky thoughts that interrupt your focus. Combat this by creating a dedicated space for visualization where you're less likely to be disturbed. Consider using background sounds, such as gentle waves or tranquil music, to help maintain your concentration. Another obstacle might be skepticism, as people wonder if this practice really works. Remember, like any skill, visualization grows stronger with practice. Trust the process and permit yourself to explore without judgment.

Visualization can be transformative, but it's important to approach it with patience. It might not seem like much at first, but over time, you'll notice subtle shifts in how you perceive and interact with the world around you. This practice isn't about creating unrealistic fantasies; it's about aligning your inner world with your outer reality. Keep in mind that the imagery you make in your mind can influence how you navigate life's challenges and opportunities.

Visualization can be a deeply personal practice unique to each individual's spiritual path. It's not about following a strict formula but rather embracing what resonates with your soul. Whether you find solace in guided imagery or inspiration from vision boards, the key is to remain open to the experience. By nurturing this practice, you invite creativity and intuition into your spiritual journey, allowing new insights and opportunities to unfold naturally.

If you're new to visualization or seeking to deepen your practice, approach it with curiosity rather than expectation. Set aside time each day to explore different techniques and observe how they impact your mindset and emotions. Be gentle with yourself if distractions arise—acknowledge them and refocus on the imagery you've crafted. Over time, you'll find that visualization becomes not just a tool for spiritual growth but an integral part of how you engage with the world.

As you continue to explore these techniques, remember that visualization is just as much about the journey as it is about the destination. Allow yourself the freedom to experiment and adapt each practice to suit your needs and aspirations. Trust that by nurturing this connection between mind and spirit, you're fostering a deeper understanding of yourself and the universe around you.

Sacred Rituals for Modern Living

Wake up each morning to a small, meaningful ritual that sets the tone for your day. Rituals imbue life with a sacred quality, creating a structure for spiritual exploration that otherwise might feel untethered. They act as a bridge between the mundane and the mystical, grounding us in the present while allowing our spirits to soar. In modern life, these rituals don't have to be grand or elaborate; they can be as simple as lighting a candle or whispering a prayer of gratitude. These small acts carry weight, turning ordinary moments into sacred experiences.

Consider the power of a morning gratitude ceremony. As you sip your morning coffee or tea, take a moment to reflect on three things you're grateful for. Feel the warmth of the cup in your hands and let that warmth spread through your body. This practice not only cultivates appreciation but also sets a positive tone for the rest of your day. It's a gentle reminder that even in the midst of chaos, blessings abound. Similarly, an evening reflection ritual invites you to review your day with mindful awareness. As you lie in bed, consider the moments that brought joy and those that challenged you. Breathe deeply, acknowledge what you've experienced, and offer gratitude for the lessons learned.

Creating personalized rituals can deepen your connection to your spiritual beliefs and values. Begin by choosing elements that resonate with you—symbols, words, or actions that hold meaning. Perhaps you have a favorite poem that inspires you or a crystal that feels grounding in your hand. Incorporate these into your rituals, allowing them to serve as anchors for your practice. Remember, rituals are intensely personal; they should reflect who you are and what you cherish.

Cultural influences can also enrich modern rituals by bringing diversity and depth to your practice. Many traditional practices can be adapted to fit contemporary contexts, thereby bridging the gap between the old and the new. For example, suppose you're drawn to Eastern philosophies. In that case, you might incorporate elements of Zen meditation or Tibetan singing bowls into your routine. Alternatively, if Indigenous practices resonate with you, consider incorporating nature walks or honoring the four directions into your ritual.

The beauty of rituals lies in their adaptability. They're not static but evolve with you, reflecting shifts in your beliefs and experiences over time. As you explore different cultural traditions, allow yourself to be inspired by their richness and creativity. This exploration not only broadens your spiritual horizons but also fosters a sense of unity across cultures, a reminder that we are all part of a larger tapestry.

It's important to approach rituals with an open heart and mind. There's no right or wrong way to engage with them; what matters is the intention behind each action. Approach each ritual with curiosity and playfulness, allowing yourself the freedom to experiment and adapt as needed. If something doesn't resonate, feel free to modify it or try something new.

Rituals can be woven seamlessly into daily life, offering moments of pause and reflection amid the hustle and bustle. They encourage us to slow down and reconnect with our inner selves, a vital practice in a world that often demands constant motion. Whether it's lighting a candle at sunrise or taking a mindful breath before bed, these small acts nourish the soul and remind us of the sacredness inherent in everyday life.

As you explore these sacred rituals for modern living, remember that they are not about perfection but presence. Embrace each moment as an opportunity for connection, both within yourself and with the world around you. Allow rituals to become touchstones for your spiritual journey, a source of inspiration and grounding amid life's ebb and flow.

Journaling for Mystical Insight

Sit down with a blank piece of paper and a pen; be ready to pour your thoughts and feelings onto the paper. Journaling can be a powerful tool for spiritual development, offering a space where you can clarify your thoughts, track your progress, and deepen your insights. It's not just about recording daily events; it's about documenting your experiences and emotions in a way that reveals patterns and truths you might not have noticed otherwise. Reflective writing enables you to explore your inner landscape, gaining a deeper understanding of your reactions and emotions with honesty and compassion. It's like having a conversation with yourself, one where you can be completely open without fear of judgment.

There are several journaling techniques you can try to see what resonates with you. Stream-of-consciousness writing involves letting your thoughts flow freely onto the page without editing or censoring yourself. This method encourages authenticity, capturing the raw essence of your thoughts as they occur. Alternatively, thematic journals focus on specific spiritual themes or questions, guiding your exploration in a more structured way. You might dedicate one journal to questions about purpose or another to dreams, allowing each entry to build on the last.

To establish a consistent journaling practice, set aside a specific time and place for writing. It could be in the morning when your mind is fresh or in the evening as a way to reflect on the day. Creating a dedicated space for journaling signals to your brain that it's time to tune out distractions and tune into yourself. Consider using prompts to inspire deeper exploration. Questions like "What am I grateful for today?" or "What challenges have I faced recently?" can guide your writing and encourage introspection.

Journaling has the transformative potential to lead to profound personal growth and spiritual awakening. By regularly documenting your thoughts and experiences, you'll start to notice recurring themes and patterns in your life—patterns that may reveal areas for growth or aspects of yourself that require attention. This awareness can lead to deeper understanding and acceptance of who you are, fostering a sense of peace and purpose.

Tracking patterns in your journal entries can also help you identify growth areas. You might notice how certain situations trigger specific emotions or how your responses have evolved over time. This insight allows you to approach challenges with greater wisdom and resilience. As you continue writing, journaling becomes a trusted companion on your spiritual path. This tool helps you navigate life's complexities with clarity and grace.

Reflect on how journaling fits into your spiritual practice. It doesn't require hours of writing; even a few minutes each day can make a significant impact. Approach it with curiosity and openness, allowing yourself the freedom to explore different techniques until you find what resonates most. Remember, there's no right or wrong way to journal. What matters is that it serves as a space for genuine self-reflection and growth.

It's clear that practical mysticism offers accessible ways to enhance spiritual exploration in everyday life. Whether through meditation, mindful breathing, visualization, rituals, or journaling, each practice invites you to connect with yourself and the world around you on a deeper level. As we move forward into the next chapter, we'll explore how integrating these practices can lead to meaningful transformation and greater fulfillment in all aspects of life. Keep an open heart and mind as you continue this journey of discovery and growth.

Chapter Six

Integrating Mysticism and Science

The Science of Meditation and Brainwaves

The journey of exploring meditation and its transformative influence on brainwaves is a captivating one. Consider the gradual tuning of a complex orchestral symphony, where each instrument quietly finds its place. In much the same way, meditation orchestrates the intricate symphony of your brainwaves, harmonizing your internal state. This process is not just like tuning into a cosmic radio station but a deep, sustainable alignment of your mind and body, leading to profound changes in your cognitive and emotional landscapes.

Delve deeper into the science of alpha waves, those serene rhythms reminiscent of a gentle brook flowing through lush woodlands. This delicate state is where balance reigns, where clarity and tranquility intermingle, and where you're neither too tense nor too lax. The beauty of alpha waves is their ability to transform mere daydreams into a canvas of stillness and creativity. Your mind floats softly, like autumn leaves on a crisp breeze, allowing you to weave through the threads of thought and mindfulness with ease and precision, leaving you feeling relaxed and at ease.

Then there are the theta waves, beckoning you like an ancient lullaby, calling forth the dormant intuitive powers within. Here is where you can sit on the cusp of consciousness and the subconscious. Envision your mind as a vast, untamed forest teeming with untapped potential and uncharted territories. Within this landscape, creative sprites flutter about, nurturing new ideas and untethered possibilities. It is during these deeper states of meditation that transformative insights burst forth like wildflowers after a spring rain, lending clarity and breadth to the challenges that we face in our daily lives.

Embracing the scientific revelations of meditation extends beyond the experiential realm. We find that neuroplasticity, the brain's remarkable ability to reshape itself, plays a pivotal role. It's as if your brain is an artist, and meditation empowers it with a palette enriched with rich oils and vibrant colors, allowing it to paint fresher, clearer, and more intricate connections. Consequently, this has a positive impact on areas such as the prefrontal cortex, with implications that include not only heightened attention but also enhanced emotional intelligence and resilience.

Furthermore, meditation is a powerful tool for fostering mental well-being. It lowers cortisol, the hormone associated with stress, while simultaneously regulating emotions. This subtractive process acts as a Sentinel, guarding your inner peace and acting as a balm against life's chaotic currents. By bringing focus and concentration into clear relief, meditation provides the tools to traverse life's intricate webs efficiently and smoothly.

Consciousness Studies for Mystical Insights in Neuroscience

Take, for instance, Mindfulness-Based Stress Reduction (MBSR), a portal that marries mindfulness with bodily awareness, providing a haven of sorts amidst life's tumultuous seas. It guides you on a journey, allowing you to cultivate a balanced approach to life's myriad challenges. In parallel, Loving-Kindness Meditation, an act of silent generosity, sows seeds of compassion and empathy, which blossom into field-encouraging harmony. It's an invitation to encompass oneself—and others—with boundless love and kindness, forging deeper, more meaningful connections.

Exploring Meditation Practices

- **Begin with Intention:** Start by formulating a purpose for your practice now and observe how this intention unfolds. It could be as simple as seeking inner peace or delving into a quest for insight, a beacon for your focus.

- **Experiment with Techniques:** Allow yourself the latitude to navigate through various meditation pathways. Experiment with different styles, each one a distinct color in your paintbrush, adding unique shades to your experiential canvas.

- **Observe the Effects:** By taking mindful note of the subtle changes in your emotions and focus from one session to the next, you will glean insights into how meditation weaves itself through your life's tapestry.

Through meditation's gentle embrace, you embark on a journey toward self-discovery, a trajectory marked by infinite expansion and growth. Dedicate just moments each day, like planting a single seed within the fertile soil. Over time, observe as it shoots forth tendrils of growth, penetrating the world, guided by the stability and anchoring of your meditative practice. This potential for personal development through meditation should leave you feeling hopeful and optimistic about the future.

As you continue to explore the realms of meditation and brainwave science, embrace the wonder of unfolding truths as they reveal themselves. Meditation is not merely a reprieve; it's a conduit, connecting you to the depths of your inner world and expanding your understanding of the external one. Approach this elegant labyrinth of self with curiosity and openness, knowing that the silent voices of insight await to guide you toward untapped potential ignited with each mindful breath.

The Enigmatic Terrain of Consciousness

Picture the metaphor of a vibrant, ever-bustling metropolis as a representation of the intricacies of the human mind. As neuroscientists venture into this city, they endeavor to distill clarity from the enigma of consciousness, much like skilled archaeologists piecing together remnants of a lost civilization. The "hard problem" within this realm pertains to the perennial mystery of subjective experiences, those intimate, deeply personal sensations that color our existence. Consider, for example, the intoxicating aroma of freshly brewed coffee wafting through the morning air, invoking not just simple pleasure but a cascade of complex feelings and memories. Such experiences are quintessentially linked to consciousness and raise profound questions: Why is music capable of evoking such intense emotions as tears or euphoria? What networks within our neural metropolis whisper these emotional narratives to us? These questions rest at the very core of consciousness studies and serve as intellectual magnets that have attracted philosophers and scientists alike through the ages.

Neuroscientific advances have led to the identification of neural correlates of consciousness, wherein specific brain regions are intricately tied to the conscious experience. Envision these sections as iconic landmarks within our mental cityscape—the formidable prefrontal cortex as the legislative center where judgments and strategies are drafted and debated, or the thalamus as the central hub, orchestrating a ceaseless flow of sensory traffic. It's like peering at a city's action from above, discerning the patterns and rhythms unseen to the pedestrian eye. During conscious states, these neural beacons glow brightly with activity, yet in altered states, such as the depths of slumber or through induced mystical states, these lights dim, offering a unique map of our internal world. This understanding not only charts where consciousness occurs but stirs curiosity about the shifts in landscapes within our psyche during different states of awareness.

Ramifications of Mystical Experiences

Try seeing mystical experiences as abandoned, less-traveled pathways weaving through this cognitive city. During such profound states, the brain's default mode network, which is often a bastion of self-referential thoughts and identity narratives, reduces its activity. This is akin to a city-wide power-down, leading to an atmospheric shift from frenetic busyness to tranquil calm. This reduction can facilitate transcendent experiences, mirroring the serene stillness experienced when gazing from a skyscraper, seeing the city not as fragmented boroughs but as a cohesive, living organism. Interestingly, research into temporal lobe epilepsy, for instance, shines a light on how involuntary disruptions can sometimes lead to intensely spiritual delves, offering clues to the conditions that might trigger such states.

As we look deeper into the intersection of neuroscience and mysticism, the concept of non-local consciousness emerges, a challenging yet exhilarating idea. This idea provocatively supposes that consciousness might transcend the tangible constraints of our neural cityscape, reaching out like ethereal tendrils into a boundless cosmic web of awareness. Think of our consciousness not merely as an isolated neuron but as a vibrant part of a vast, expansive archipelago connected by invisible cognitive bridges crafted from transient thoughts and collective experiences.

Bridging Science and Mysticism

The implications are as profound as they are extraordinary. Consciousness studies suggest that mystical experiences may not simply exist as isolated hallucinations or psychological anomalies but rather as genuine reflections of an interconnected reality. This realization prompts further inquiry into how individual consciousness can tap into a collective, transcendent awareness that transcends the immediate physical boundaries of brain cells and neurons.

Looking forward, the potential of unfolding research to bridge the gap further between the ethereal visions of mysticism and the concrete rigor of science is genuinely compelling. Emerging technologies, such as sophisticated brain-computer interfaces, offer tantalizing possibilities—imagine capturing the real-time electrical symphony of the brain during mystical states, unlocking the secrets of these profound experiences. Such tools could revolutionize both neuroscientific inquiry and spiritual exploration, fostering a dialogue between once divergent disciplines.

In this compelling journey, we should embrace a dual sense of respect and inquisitiveness, acknowledging both the established truths of modern discovery and the vast unknowns that remain to be explored. Journeying into this domain is not a quest for finite answers but a celebration of the intricate and breathtaking complexity of human experience. It is an acknowledgment that our mental cities harbor boundless trails awaiting discovery, promising new vistas of understanding and interconnection.

Science and mysticism, rather than serving as opposing forces, can merge as partners, both striving to unravel the grand mysteries of life. The integration of insights from these realms will pave the way for a more enriched understanding of consciousness and its pivotal role in shaping the human experience. Whether dissecting neurons under a microscope or reflecting on the universe under a celestial canopy, we find common threads in our quest to uncover the deepest aspects of what it means to be conscious entities in this marvelous, continually unfolding universe. Through this shared pursuit, we deepen our understanding of ourselves and the cosmos, and in doing so, we light the path toward greater harmony and insight.

Quantum Physics and Mystical Reality

You're standing at the edge of a vast ocean, where the waves gently kiss the shore, each whispering secrets of the universe. Quantum physics, much like this ocean, reveals a world teeming with mysteries. At its heart is the concept of wave-particle duality, a term that may sound complex but is surprisingly straightforward. Picture particles behaving like waves, spreading across space, and then suddenly acting like solid objects when observed. It's as if the universe is in a constant dance of being and becoming, never quite settling into one form. This duality resonates with mystical traditions that speak of reality as fluid and ever-changing, blurring the lines between the seen and the unseen.

But it doesn't stop there. Enter quantum entanglement, where particles become so intertwined that the actions of one instantaneously affect the other, regardless of distance. It's like having two friends separated by miles but knowing instinctively what the other feels. This concept mirrors the mystical idea of interconnectedness, suggesting that everything in the universe is connected in ways we can't always perceive. It's a reminder that even in our solitude, we are never truly alone.

Now, consider the philosophical interpretations of quantum mechanics that align with mystical thought. The observer effect, for instance, tells us that the act of observing can influence reality itself. It's a mind-bending notion, just by looking, you're changing what you see. This aligns with the mystical belief that consciousness shapes our experiences and that reality is not a fixed entity but a dynamic interplay between perception and existence.

Bohm's implicate order takes this further by suggesting that the universe is an interconnected whole, with everything enfolded into everything else. Imagine a hologram where each piece contains the whole image, no matter how small. In this view, separation is an illusion; everything is part of a larger tapestry. It echoes ancient mystical teachings that speak of unity and oneness, urging us to look beyond superficial divisions.

Yet, this intersection of quantum physics and mysticism sparks spirited debates. Critics argue that quantum mysticism is often misused or misinterpreted, pointing out that not all claims withstand scientific scrutiny. They warn against bending scientific principles to fit mystical narratives, emphasizing the importance of maintaining scientific rigor and objectivity. Despite these debates, the allure of quantum mysticism persists, inviting us to explore its possibilities while acknowledging its limitations.

To illustrate this intersection, let's examine Schrödinger's cat, a famous thought experiment that captures the strangeness of quantum mechanics. Imagine a cat in a sealed box with a mechanism that can release poison based on a random quantum event. Until observed, the cat exists in a state of both alive and dead. This paradox serves as a metaphor for mystical understanding, where reality transcends binary oppositions and simultaneously embraces multiple truths.

Through these concepts and debates, quantum physics offers insights that resonate deeply with mystical ideas. It challenges us to rethink our notions of reality and to embrace uncertainty as an integral part of the human experience. The universe is not merely a machine ticking away predictably; it's a vibrant, mysterious dance inviting us to join in and explore its depths.

As we ponder these connections, it's essential to approach them with curiosity and an open mind. Quantum physics is not about providing definitive answers but about expanding our understanding of what's possible. It encourages us to see beyond conventional boundaries and explore new ways of thinking about reality.

In this exploration of quantum physics and mysticism, we find a shared quest for understanding, a desire to uncover hidden patterns and reveal more profound truths about existence. Whether through science or spirituality, both paths offer glimpses into the profound interconnectedness that binds us all.

While these ideas may seem abstract or complex at first glance, they invite us to engage with them on a personal level. They remind us that we are part of something greater than ourselves, like a vast, intricate web where each thread contributes to the whole. As we continue our journey through this chapter, let these insights inspire you to reflect on your own experiences and connections within this ever-unfolding tapestry.

Quantum physics and mysticism together paint a picture of reality filled with wonder and potential; a world where paradoxes coexist harmoniously and where every observation is an invitation to explore further. In embracing these ideas with an open heart and mind, we embark on a path of discovery that enriches our understanding of ourselves and our place in the universe.

This exploration is not about reaching conclusions but about deepening our appreciation for life's mysteries—an invitation to dance with uncertainty and celebrate the beauty found in connection and unity.

Bridging the Gap Between Mysticism and Psychology

The intersection of psychology and mysticism provides a profound and intensely fascinating lens through which we can critically examine and gain a deeper understanding of mystical experiences, shedding remarkable light on how these extraordinary occurrences shape our inner worlds in complex and intricate ways. Carl Jung's pioneering theories, for instance, offer a compellingly insightful framework for a deep understanding of the multifaceted psychological dimensions of mystical experiences. Jung introduced the concept of archetypes, universal symbols and motifs that magnificently surface in dreams, myths, and, indeed, intriguing mystical states. These transcendent archetypes serve as a vital bridge, connecting the conscious and unconscious mind, and offer genuine and profound insights into our deepest fears, desires, and spiritual longings. For instance, you might encounter the Wise Old Man or the Great Mother in your dreams or visions, symbolizing wisdom, guidance, or nurturing aspects of the psyche, respectively. Recognizing these symbolic elements within mystical experiences can illuminate overlooked aspects of your psyche that are earnestly seeking attention or yearning for transformation.

In a similar vein, Abraham Maslow's concept of peak experiences closely aligns with mystical states, further revealing the connection between psychological states and spiritual experiences. These are not just fleeting moments but rather moments of intense, sometimes overwhelming clarity and transcendence, where you feel an incredible sense of unity with the universe or profound insight into life's perennial mysteries. Maslow described them as life's high points, often accompanied by feelings of joy, creativity, and an unshakeable sense of connectedness. These peak experiences are not merely transient sensations; they imprint deeply on the psyche, leaving lasting impressions that can profoundly reshape your worldview and inspire personal growth and evolution. Integrating these insightful lessons into daily life can lead to a deeper understanding of yourself and your significant place in the world.

Mystical practices have intriguingly found their way into therapeutic settings, offering intriguing healing avenues that surpass traditional methods. Transpersonal psychology, for example, acknowledges spiritual experiences as integral and central to mental health. It views the psyche as inherently spiritual and intricately seeks to integrate these potentially transformative experiences into therapy. This approach allows individuals to explore their unique spiritual identities, facilitating healing through the acceptance and understanding of their mystical experiences. It's fundamentally about recognizing that spirituality is not separate from mental health but is a vital, interconnected component of it.

Mindfulness-Based Cognitive Therapy (MBCT) is another notable example of this integration, combining cognitive therapy with mindfulness practices in a meticulous manner. This therapeutic approach earnestly encourages you to observe your thoughts and feelings without judgment, fostering a conscious sense of detachment from negative thought patterns. Through mindfulness practices like meditation, breath awareness, and mindful observation, you promote a greater resilience against stress and anxiety. This fusion of cognitive and spiritual practices not only alleviates psychological distress but also nurtures a deeper connection to your inner self, promoting a profound sense of well-being and clarity.

Altered states of consciousness, another intriguing domain, play a pivotal role in psychological healing by facilitating introspection, self-reflection, and personal growth. Flow states—those immersive, timeless moments when you become completely absorbed in an engaging activity are a prime example. Whether you're painting, playing music, or even gardening, these states wonderfully allow you to lose track of time and self-consciousness, naturally creating space for creativity and insight to flourish spontaneously. Flow states promote well-being by fostering a sense of purpose and achievement, enhancing your overall quality of life and sense of fulfillment.

To weave psychological insights into mystical practice involves implementing practical and adaptable strategies that enrich and invigorate both realms in a meaningful way. Self-reflection exercises are invaluable tools for achieving personal insight, transformation, and clarity. Consider keeping a journal where you explore your thoughts and emotions freely, passionately, and without censorship. This practice encourages self-awareness by allowing you to observe and analyze recurring patterns or themes manifesting in your life. Reflective writing can also help you process mystical experiences more deeply, often revealing underlying messages, insights, or lessons that may have been overlooked.

Active imagination is another profoundly powerful technique that engages the unconscious mind for expansive spiritual exploration. This practice involves visualizing dialogues or interactions with inner figures or symbols encountered in dreams or meditations. By openly engaging with these elements, you can gain new insights into unresolved issues or unanswered questions in your life. Active imagination encourages a dynamic dialogue between conscious awareness and the unconscious mind, ultimately facilitating greater understanding, discovery, and personal growth.

As we thoughtfully conclude this comprehensive and expansive chapter on bridging mysticism with psychology, it's distinctly clear that both fields offer rich, layered insights into the human experience. By integrating these disciplines, we can deepen our understanding of ourselves while fostering holistic spiritual growth and psychological well-being. As we seamlessly transition into the next chapter, let's continue exploring how science and spirituality intersect in unexpected ways to enrich and illuminate our lives in fulfilling and holistic ways.

Chapter Seven

Overcoming Challenges on the Mystical Path

Overcoming Fear and Doubt in Mystical Practices

Picture yourself standing at the edge of an expansive, enchanting forest. The trees, ancient and majestic, rise to impressive heights, their branches forming a dense canopy above. These towering giants cast intricate shadows that shift and sway with the gentle breeze, creating a mesmerizing dance of light and dark that seems to invite and yet challenge the heart. This is your threshold, your point of embarkation, filled with wonder and a tangible air of mystery.

At this pivotal moment, you are filled with a mixture of anticipation and apprehension. You're about to venture into a realm where every step promises new discoveries. However, with this promise of profound revelations comes the potential for unexpected challenges, each turn leading to uncharted territories. This scene vividly mirrors the mystical journey, an alluring quest yet shrouded in veils of ambiguity. As you inch forward into the unknown, fear and doubt begin to whisper, posing probing questions that echo your innermost uncertainties. Could you truly encounter something that defies the logic and explanations of the well-charted world? Would it illuminate your path with transcendent knowledge, or would you find yourself in a void, lost in silence?

Such fears are intrinsic to human nature, seeds sown in the fertile soil of our desire to understand and control our reality. One of the most formidable fears is the concern over mystical experiences that defy comprehension and understanding. What awaits you in the beyond? Is it enigmatic visions, profound insights, or an echoing void? The mere thought of such experiences can quicken the heart, prompting a retreat into the safety of the known world. Another formidable doubt arises from the fear of societal judgment. In societies where spiritual practices are viewed with skepticism, one may wonder how others might perceive these exploratory pursuits. Will loved ones dismiss your spiritual journey as whimsical or misguided?

Peering into the depths of these fears can shed light on their origins. Cultural and social conditioning significantly shape our perspective, fostering skepticism toward the mystical. From childhood onward, we are often immersed in environments that uplift logic and empirical evidence over intuitive and spiritual exploration. This predisposition can create an internal battleground, where one struggles to reconcile the allure of mystical experiences with the rationality they have learned. On a deeply personal level, insecurities concerning your abilities to engage effectively in spiritual practices may give rise to doubt. Pervasive questions about "doing it right" or whether you are truly poised for significant spiritual breakthroughs can gnaw at the resolve.

How, then, does one confront this formidable amalgam of doubt and fear? Mindfulness becomes a steadfast ally, anchoring you in present awareness amid storms of anxiety. By immersing yourself fully in the current moment, you disentangle from the spiraling tendrils of uncertainty. Techniques, such as deep breathing and comprehensive body scans, soothe the tumultuous inner climate, restoring calm and focus to the overwhelmed mind (Harvard Health Publishing). Positive affirmations serve as fortifying mantras, bolstering a spirit of trust and courage. By continuously affirming, "I am open to new experiences" or "I trust my intuition," these expressions weave an empowering narrative, transforming doubt into a foundation of confidence and assurance. With mindfulness, you can navigate the unknown with a sense of reassurance.

Embracing fear is not simply about dissolving it; it metamorphoses fear into a wellspring of strength and resilience. By standing firm against these haunting specters, you cultivate tenacity and adaptability. Navigating the unpredictable paths of the mystical strengthens your determination and instills a graceful resilience that turns adversity into opportunity. Gradually, what had appeared insurmountable began to shift, unveiling a landscape pregnant with opportunities for personal and spiritual growth. With each conquest of fear, novel perspectives enrich your understanding, clearing the fog and bathed in new light. This transformation of fear into strength is a powerful journey that you can embark on.

Confronting Fear

- **Identify Your Fears:** Set aside a few minutes to write down any anxieties or misgivings you have about exploring mystical practices. Let this exercise be a gateway to acknowledging and understanding these fears.

- **Explore Their Roots:** Conduct a thoughtful reflection on the origins of these fears; how are they influenced by cultural norms or rooted in personal self-doubt?

- **Develop Strategies:** Envision how integrating mindfulness practices and affirmations might mitigate these fears and design a personalized approach.

Facing fear does not equate to its complete eradication; instead, it involves reshaping your relationship with fear. The unknown, once the harbinger of uncertainty, transforms into a landscape teeming with potential and infinite prospects. As you forge ahead on this mystical journey, cultivate the understanding that fear operates not as an impediment but as a transformative agent. This critical element propels you toward richer spiritual insights and unprecedented personal growth.

Consistency in Practice and Handling Setbacks

See yourself on a winding path leading through a dense forest. Each step you take is deliberate, marking your commitment to the mystical practices that draw you in. Just as walking this path requires dedication, consistency, and a willingness to keep moving forward even when the trail becomes challenging, so too does regular spiritual practice. The importance of consistency cannot be overstated. It's the backbone of spiritual growth, the thread that weaves your intentions into your daily life. Building habits is akin to laying bricks; each small effort contributes to a sturdy foundation upon which you can stand.

In the realm of spiritual practices, incremental progress is your ally. Imagine a potter at their wheel, shaping clay into a vessel. Each rotation, each touch, brings the form closer to completion. Similarly, each session of meditation, prayer, or contemplation adds to your spiritual journey. Over time, these seemingly small efforts accumulate into a tapestry of growth and understanding. This cumulative effect is where the magic happens—not in grand gestures but in the quiet persistence of daily practice.

Yet, even with the best intentions, setbacks can disrupt the rhythm of your spiritual practice. Balancing responsibilities can feel like a high-wire act, where time for reflection competes with obligations. On some days, finding a moment for meditation amidst a whirlwind of tasks might seem impossible. Then there's the challenge of motivation, a force as unpredictable as the weather. One day, you're eager and inspired; the next, you might feel as though you're wading through mud, with apathy dragging at your heels.

So, how do you navigate these obstacles without losing momentum? Start by setting realistic goals. Define what you want to achieve in your practice, but ensure these goals are attainable within your current lifestyle. Instead of aiming for an hour-long meditation session, start with ten minutes each day. Small steps pave the way for lasting change and reduce the risk of burnout. Finding an accountability partner can also be a game-changer. Connect with someone who shares your commitment to spiritual growth. Share your goals and check in regularly. Together, you'll create an environment of mutual support and encouragement.

Setbacks are not failures; they are a natural part of life's ebb and flow. Embrace them as opportunities for reflection and adjustment. Consider them like waves on a beach; they may pull back temporarily but eventually return with renewed strength. When you encounter a setback, please take a moment to evaluate why it occurred. Was it due to external circumstances or perhaps a shift in your own needs? Use this reflection to adapt your practices accordingly.

Lastly, embrace imperfection as part of your spiritual journey. Perfection is an illusion that can lead to frustration and self-doubt when not attained. Instead of striving for flawlessness, allow yourself to be human. Accept that some days will be easier than others and that every effort, regardless of perceived success, contributes to your growth. Like a musician learning a new piece, there will be moments of discord before harmony emerges.

Navigating Setbacks

- **Identify Recent Setbacks:** Reflect on any recent obstacles you've faced in maintaining your spiritual practice. Consider how they made you feel and why they might have occurred.

- **Adaptation Strategies:** Consider how you can adjust your practice to better align with your current lifestyle. Could you incorporate shorter sessions or explore new techniques?

- **Reframe Your Perspective:** Shift your focus from perfection to progress. Celebrate small victories and remind yourself that each effort brings you closer to your spiritual goals.

By embracing setbacks as integral components of your journey, you cultivate resilience and adaptability—qualities that not only enhance your spiritual growth but also improve your ability to navigate life's broader challenges with greater ease and poise.

Finding Your Spiritual Community

Consider a scenario where you are enveloped by people who truly resonate with your core essence. It's an atmosphere where shared ideas germinate like seeds of potential, becoming a nurturing ground for mutual growth and understanding. Being part of a spiritual community manifests this vision into reality, akin to discovering your tribe. This group offers not only insights and knowledge but also a profound sense of belonging and warmth. Picture yourself seated in a welcoming circle, an assemblage of individuals sharing their diverse and unique experiences. Each story is a tapestry woven with lessons learned and insights gained, carrying with it an energy that contributes to the collective wisdom of the group. This shared database of wisdom does more than enrich your knowledge; it intricately layers and deepens your spiritual practice. The exchange is far more than a mere swapping of stories; it is a holistic absorption of the collective intelligence and understanding that spans diverse backgrounds and myriad spiritual paths, all converging to provide a multifaceted view, enabling you to perceive things from new perspectives.

However, the essence of a spiritual community transcends mere learning; it encompasses the reassuring experience of being acknowledged and understood. During trying times, this community manifests as your anchor, providing an emotional safety net that catches and cradles you when life pitches its inevitable curveballs. Picture the comfort of knowing that there are others ready to offer steadfast encouragement or a sympathetic ear, especially when you find yourself traversing challenges or experiencing solitude in your journey. The fortitude derived from such support can be genuinely transformative, morphing obstacles into stepping stones and weaknesses into strengths.

So, how does one embark on the journey of discovering or forming such a community? Initial steps may include exploring online spiritual forums. These virtual oases connect you with like-minded souls scattered across the globe, individuals who share your passion and can offer encouragement from afar. The internet provides a vast array of platforms dedicated to spirituality, serving as vibrant gathering places for engaging discussions and enlightening exchanges. Whether through social media groups or specialized spiritual websites, these forums serve as an invaluable resource for finding like-minded individuals, all without leaving the comfort of your own home.

For those who relish face-to-face interaction, local meetups provide golden opportunities to connect with individuals enthused about spirituality right within your geographical vicinity. Some postings may be found at local community centers or libraries, where bulletin boards often advertise spiritual gatherings. Spaces such as yoga studios, meditation centers, and bookstores frequently host events or workshops that appeal to spiritually minded individuals. Attending these functions can be a delightful way to encounter others who share your values and interests, foster connections, and deepen your spiritual journey.

Once you've pinpointed a prospective community, it's crucial to ascertain whether it aligns with your values and objectives. Seek out hallmarks that define a healthy spiritual community. Inclusivity and openness are fundamental; a welcoming atmosphere ensures that diverse perspectives are not only accepted but celebrated. This implies that people hailing from various backgrounds and holding different beliefs should feel at ease sharing their experiences sans fear of judgment. Such diversity injects life into the community's fabric, rendering it vibrant and dynamic with a colorful array of perspectives and ideas.

Mutual respect constitutes a primary pillar of a thriving community. Every member's contributions must be esteemed equally. A space that attaches value to every voice helps cultivate an environment of trust and collaboration. Observing how group leaders facilitate discussions can offer insights into whether the community truly upholds these principles mentioned above. Nevertheless, involvement in any group setting may present its own set of challenges. Group dynamics occasionally lead to conflicts or diverging opinions, which, although natural, require careful navigation. Navigating these scenarios with patience and an open mind is crucial. Equipping oneself with practical communication skills can help manage disagreements constructively, converting potential tension into opportunities for deeper understanding and growth.

A further challenge lies in maintaining personal boundaries amid communal activities. It's easy to become swept up in the collective enthusiasm of the group and momentarily forget one's individuality. Still, it's vital to remember and honor your unique path. Being a part of a community doesn't imply conforming to every idea or perspective presented; instead, it's about striking a harmonious balance between embracing collective wisdom and staying true to your personal beliefs and spiritual integrity.

Being part of a spiritual community involves more than merely attending meetings or participating in discussions; it's about engaging deeply with others who tread similar paths while simultaneously carving out your niche within that collective journey. The connections you establish can be transformative, providing the essential support needed during challenging times and the inspiration to continue exploring uncharted realms on your spiritual journey.

Balancing Material and Spiritual Lives

Your life is an expansive, intricate tapestry, where each thread intricately weaves together to symbolize the varied roles you embody every single day, such as being a nurturing parent, a dedicated worker, a supportive friend, and a seeker of knowledge and truth. We often find ourselves ensnared in the complex tension between the tangible responsibilities of the material world and our spiritual aspirations, much like endeavoring to balance precariously on a tightrope while juggling flaming torches that threaten to tip the balance with every misstep. It is, without a doubt, a remarkable feat to harmonize these seemingly competing demands. Yet, it is within this delicate dance between the material world that tethers us and the spiritual realm that beckons us that the true magic of life begins to unfold. Meeting stringent deadlines and responsibilities at work can often feel akin to navigating a whirlwind, even as your soul whispers a quiet call for reflection, yearning for moments of peace and introspection.

The challenge of integrating spiritual practices into the fabric of everyday life often resembles a strenuous tug-of-war, with demands pulling in one direction, seeking acknowledgment. In contrast, spiritual aspirations tug in the opposite direction, whispering a call to connection with a greater purpose. At one end of the rope, there are pressing job demands, bills waiting to be paid, and family obligations that require our utmost attention. On the other hand, lies an undeniable yearning for spiritual growth, a profound desire to connect with something greater, transcending beyond the self. Striking this elusive balance is reminiscent of trying to hold water in cupped hands; it unfailingly seems to escape just when it appears secure. Nevertheless, prioritizing time for spiritual activities need not be about unearthing more hours in the day but rather about making conscious choices that resonate deeply with your values and essence. It may entail choosing a serene early morning meditation over mindless scrolling through your phone or opting for a contemplative walk through nature instead of indulging in a marathon TV session.

When you earnestly adopt a balanced approach to life, the cumulative benefits extend their gentle ripples through every facet of your existence, much like a serene breeze. Enhanced well-being remains one of the most significant rewards, as engaging in regular spiritual practices can profoundly improve mental and emotional health by diminishing stress and fostering resilience. Such practices act like an emotional safety net, one that cradles and supports you when life throws its unpredictable curveballs. Greater fulfillment naturally follows as you begin to experience satisfaction and contentment in both the material and spiritual realms. Visualize, if you will, the joy of feeling contentment in your career pursuits while simultaneously savoring profound moments of spiritual insight—a genuine sense that you are living authentically and to the fullest of your potential.

Strategies for achieving the balance between material and spiritual endeavors require practical, actionable tools and a mindful, intentional approach. Time management techniques become essential for facilitating effective scheduling across all realms of your life. Consider employing planners or digital calendars to assign dedicated time slots for your work tasks, family commitments, and deeply enriching spiritual practices. This structured approach ensures that each area receives the necessary attention without overwhelming the pace of your schedule. Mindful transitions are equally important when shifting focus from one task to another. Practicing deep, centering breaths or setting intentional, mindful transitions before moving from work mode to meditation facilitates smoother, more harmonious transitions.

The transformative potential of living a balanced life is profound, leading to holistic growth and sustained inner peace. Nurturing all dimensions of your being—whether physical, emotional, mental, or spiritual—cultivates a unique sense of wholeness that radiates outward, weaving itself into every interaction. Holistic growth involves recognizing that each segment of your life is intricately interconnected, where nurturing one enriches the others. Achieving sustained inner peace does not inherently mean eliminating life's challenges but approaching them with newfound calmness, clarity, and understanding.

Living a balanced life facilitates and invites personal and spiritual transformation by nurturing deeper, more meaningful connections with yourself and those around you. It fosters greater self-awareness and understanding, empowering you to navigate life's challenges with grace while wholeheartedly embracing opportunities for growth and enrichment. As you continue your exploratory journey through these themes throughout this book, keep in mind that balance is not synonymous with perfection; instead, it's about creating a harmonious integration of all facets of your life.

Reflect upon how these insights enhance your path toward greater fulfillment and holistic growth. In the forthcoming chapter, we shall delve into practical strategies for deepening your mystical experiences even further, a step closer to uncovering the extraordinary beauty within the ordinary moments of day-to-day life.

Chapter Eight

The Philosophy of Mysticism

The Ultimate Unification, Non-duality

You're standing at the edge of a vast ocean, where the horizon blurs and the sky melds with water. This scene captures the essence of non-duality—a concept that transcends the typical boundaries we draw between self and others. It whispers a truth that has been echoed across mystical traditions: the separation we perceive is an illusion. Non-duality invites us to see beyond these illusions, to recognize that the divine dwells within and around us, bridging the apparent chasm between the self and the universe. You, too, are part of this grand unity.

In Advaita Vedanta, a prominent school of Hindu philosophy, this concept is beautifully articulated. It posits that Brahman, the ultimate unchanging reality, is identical to Atman, the individual self. This perspective suggests that our authentic essence is not separate from the cosmic whole but is intrinsically linked to it (Advaita Vedanta, 2023). The realization of this oneness leads to moksha, liberation from the cycle of birth and rebirth. This understanding challenges us to perceive life through a lens of unity rather than division.

Zen Buddhism also champions this idea of transcending dualistic thought. Zen encourages practitioners to experience reality directly, without the filter of conceptual thinking. Through practices like zazen or sitting meditation, individuals learn to quiet their minds and see past the distinctions that usually dominate their perceptions. In doing so, Zen practitioners aim for satori—a profound insight or awakening into the non-dual nature of reality (Japanese Zen Buddhist Philosophy, n.d.). This practice emphasizes living in the present moment, where distractions fade away, revealing a world boundless and undivided.

The implications of embracing non-dual awareness are profound. As you begin to dissolve the ego's grip, you might discover a liberation from the confines of self-identity. The ego often acts as a barrier, separating you from others and skewing your perceptions. By letting go of this false sense of self, you're free to explore your interconnectedness with all existence. This shift can lead to what some call unity consciousness—a state where you experience life as an undivided whole. In this space, empathy and compassion naturally arise as the boundaries between self and others blur into insignificance. This transformation is not just a possibility but a powerful reality waiting to be embraced, inspiring you to live a more connected and compassionate life.

To cultivate non-dual awareness, specific practices can serve as beacons along the path. Meditation focused on oneness involves contemplating the interconnectedness of all things. You might visualize yourself as a drop in an endless ocean or imagine your breath as part of a larger rhythm that links all living beings. Such practices help dissolve the illusion of separateness and foster a sense of unity with the cosmos.

Contemplative inquiry is another powerful tool that invites you to question the nature of duality itself. This practice encourages examining one's beliefs about oneself and others, questioning their validity at every turn. As you inquire deeply into your assumptions about identity and reality, you may uncover insights that revolutionize your understanding of who you are—a being intimately connected to everything around you.

Non-dual awareness isn't just a lofty ideal for meditation mats or retreat centers; it permeates daily life in transformative ways. It can profoundly influence how you interact with others and make decisions. When you act from a place of unity consciousness, compassion becomes a natural part of your being. You begin to view others' joys and sorrows as inseparable from your own, leading to more empathetic and thoughtful interactions. This practical application of non-dual awareness empowers you to make a positive impact in your daily interactions, fostering harmony and connection wherever you go.

In practical terms, this might mean approaching conflicts with greater understanding or extending kindness without expectation of return. Such actions have ripple effects, fostering harmony and connection wherever they go.

Exploring Non-dual Awareness

- **Reflect on Moments of Connection:** Recall instances when you felt deeply connected to something larger than yourself, perhaps during a walk in nature or while creating art.

- **Contemplate Your Identity:** Question your assumptions about who you are beyond societal labels or roles.

- **Engage in Meditation:** Spend time each day focusing on your breathing or visualizing unity with all beings.

By exploring these practices and concepts further, you're invited into an expanded way of seeing—a perspective where boundaries blur and love flows freely across every divide.

Living with Awareness and Mystical Ethics

Wake up each day and feel a deep sense of connection to everything around you. Mystical ethics stems from this awareness, guiding us to live in harmony with all beings. At its heart, mystical ethics isn't just a set of rules; it's an understanding of our place in the tapestry of existence. When we see ourselves as part of a larger whole, our actions naturally align with spiritual values. This alignment isn't about rigid moral codes but about living with integrity and authenticity. Ethical living becomes a reflection of our spiritual insights, not just an obligation. It's a powerful choice we make every day.

Mystical experiences, often characterized by a profound sense of connection and unity, bring clarity and frequently shed light on ethical behavior. These moments of heightened awareness offer insights that go beyond conventional morality. They speak to moral intuition—an innate understanding of right and wrong that transcends learned behavior. In these states, the welfare of others becomes paramount. You start to see that every action has an impact, creating ripples in the vast ocean of interconnected lives. This newfound responsibility, guided by mystical experiences, encourages us to act with empathy and compassion, considering not only personal gain but the collective good.

Mystical philosophies across traditions have inspired specific ethical principles that guide behavior. One such principle is ahimsa, found in Hinduism and Buddhism, which advocates non-violence in thought, word, and deed. It's a commitment to causing no harm, recognizing that every life is sacred. Another example is Gandhi's concept of satyagraha, which emphasizes the power of truth and nonviolent resistance. It's a call to stand firmly in truth, even in the face of injustice, using love and patience as tools for change. These principles, rooted in mystical traditions, provide practical guidance for living an ethical life.

Yet, the mystical path isn't without its ethical challenges. One common dilemma is spiritual bypassing—using spirituality as an escape from difficult emotions or uncomfortable truths. It's tempting to mask pain with positivity, but actual growth requires facing these feelings head-on. Being aware of this tendency can help you stay grounded and authentic in your practice. Another challenge is the tension between authenticity and conformity. As you explore your spiritual path, you may encounter pressures to fit into predefined roles or expectations. Staying true to yourself is crucial, even when it means standing apart from the crowd.

These challenges underscore the importance of discernment on the mystical path. It's about finding the balance between honoring your unique journey and remaining open to guidance from others. Authenticity doesn't mean rejecting all influences; it means integrating them in ways that resonate deeply with who you are. Practicing honesty with yourself can help navigate these dilemmas, allowing for genuine expression without losing sight of your core values.

When we discuss mystical ethics, we refer to a way of being rooted in awareness and compassion. This perspective encourages us to reflect on the impact of our actions on ourselves and others. It enables us to live with intention, making choices that reflect our most deeply held values. And while this path isn't always easy, it's profoundly rewarding.

Ethical living through a mystical lens transforms everyday decisions into opportunities for growth and connection. Whether you're choosing how to respond in a challenging situation or deciding where to focus your energy, these choices become acts of service, not only to yourself but to the world around you. The beauty of mystical ethics lies in its simplicity; it's not about grand gestures but small, consistent acts of kindness and integrity.

By integrating these ethical principles into daily life, we create a world where love and compassion guide our interactions. It's about embodying the wisdom gained through mystical experiences, letting it shape our relationships and influence our choices. This way of living invites us into more profound harmony with all beings, fostering a sense of unity that transcends individual differences.

In embracing mystical ethics, we align our actions with spiritual insights, creating a ripple effect that extends far beyond ourselves. When we live in this place of awareness and connection, we contribute to a more compassionate and just world. Through mindful action and ethical consideration, we can nurture a reality where every choice reflects our commitment to love and truth.

This exploration of mystical ethics serves as a reminder that true spirituality isn't just about personal enlightenment; it's about how we show up for others, for the planet, and for ourselves. It's about weaving our spiritual insights into the fabric of everyday life, creating a tapestry that's rich with meaning and purpose.

So, as you continue on your path, consider how mystical ethics can inform your actions and decisions. Reflect on what it means to live with awareness and integrity, not just in moments of meditation or prayer but in every interaction you have. Let these insights guide you toward a life that's not only spiritually fulfilling but also deeply connected to the world around you.

Embrace the challenges and joys that come with this way of living, knowing that each step brings you closer to a deeper understanding of yourself and your place within the cosmic dance.

The Role of Love and Compassion in Mysticism

Feel the warmth of sunlight on your face, spreading a gentle glow that seems to touch everything around you. That's what love and compassion do in the realm of mysticism. They're not just emotions; they're foundational to spiritual growth and realization. Across mystical traditions, love—often referred to as agape or unconditional love—serves as a guiding principle. It's the kind of love that sees beyond flaws and embraces the divine in everyone. This isn't about romantic love or friendship; it's about a boundless love that connects us all, transcending boundaries and barriers and resonating with the core of our being.

In Buddhism, the practice of metta, or loving-kindness meditation, helps cultivate this quality. Metta encourages practitioners to extend warmth and goodwill first to themselves, then gradually outward to others, even those they find challenging to love. It's a practice that softens the heart, breaking down walls of resentment and misunderstanding. By focusing on phrases like "May you be happy" or "May you be free from suffering," metta meditation transforms our perception of ourselves and others, fostering empathy and connection.

Love and compassion hold transformative power. When we nurture these qualities, they ripple through our lives, bringing profound inner change. Consider relationships: when conflicts arise, empathy can be the bridge that leads to resolution. By stepping into another's shoes, we open ourselves to understanding rather than judgment. This shift not only mends but also deepens relationships, creating bonds rooted in mutual respect and care. Within ourselves, embracing love and acceptance fosters inner peace. We learn to be gentle with our imperfections, cultivating a serene heart that remains steady during life's storms.

Practices that foster love and compassion aren't confined to meditation mats—they can be woven into everyday life. Tonglen meditation, for instance, is a Tibetan Buddhist practice where you breathe in the suffering of others and breathe out relief and healing. This simple yet profound exercise expands your capacity for empathy by actively engaging with the pain of others and transforming it through your breath. Sit quietly, visualize someone in distress as you inhale their suffering, then exhale comfort and peace toward them. This practice not only cultivates compassion but also strengthens your ability to hold space for others in their times of need.

Compassionate listening is another powerful approach. In a world often filled with noise and distraction, offering someone your full attention becomes an act of love. It means setting aside your agenda and truly hearing what the other person is sharing. This kind of listening isn't about crafting a response or solving problems; it's about being fully present, validating their experience without judgment. By creating a safe space for vulnerability and expression, compassionate listening fosters deep, healing, and empowering connections.

The societal implications of widespread compassion are profound. Imagine communities where compassion is the norm—communities where people feel seen, valued, and respected, regardless of their background or beliefs. Such environments foster inclusivity, breaking down barriers that divide us. When compassion becomes a collective value, it influences broader social dynamics, encouraging cooperation over competition and understanding over conflict.

Community building thrives on these principles. When individuals come together with a shared commitment to empathy and kindness, they create supportive networks that uplift everyone involved. These communities become havens where people can explore their spirituality without fear of judgment or exclusion. They become places where differences are celebrated rather than tolerated—where diversity enriches rather than divides.

As compassion spreads, it reshapes societal structures, promoting policies and practices that prioritize well-being over profit or power. In education, it means creating environments where students feel safe and secure enough to express themselves authentically. In the workplace, it means creating cultures that value collaboration and support rather than cutthroat competition.

Love and compassion aren't just personal qualities; they're catalysts for transformation at every level—from individual lives to entire societies. They encourage us to see beyond ourselves, recognizing our interconnectedness with all beings. When we fully embrace these qualities, we contribute to a world that's more harmonious, equitable, and just—a world where every action reflects our shared humanity.

In nurturing love and compassion within ourselves, we become agents of change in the world around us. We create ripples that extend far beyond our immediate circles—ripples that inspire others to do the same. Through simple acts of kindness and understanding each day, we weave threads of love into the fabric of existence—a tapestry rich in meaning and beauty that will last for generations yet to come.

Philosophical Reflections on the Nature of Reality

Imagine waking up in a world where every sight you witness and sensation you feel is merely part of an intricately crafted theater, a grand spectacle of illusion designed to occupy your senses and intellect. This fascinating notion reaches beyond the realm of science fiction and into the heart of mystical traditions that span centuries. Among such beliefs is a profoundly engaging concept from Hindu philosophy, known as "Maya." This intriguing idea suggests that the tangible world we navigate is much like the thin veil of a masquerade, obscuring a deeper, ultimate reality that rests just beyond our everyday awareness. Maya does not imply that the physical world is devoid of significance. Instead, it beckons us to recognize the superficiality of mere appearances. It challenges us to engage in a more profound contemplation of existence.

Turning to Buddhism, we see a parallel examination of the world's elusive nature in the concept of "Shunyata," or emptiness. The teachings of the Buddha invite us to grapple with the understanding that nothing possesses an inherent, standalone existence. This principle is not meant to assert that things are absent but rather to highlight their conditional state – existence interwoven with the myriad factors that contribute to their being. Envision this as akin to observing the cosmos from a viewpoint of infinite interconnections, understanding that nothing exists in isolation. Embracing the notion of emptiness can liberate us from the chains of attachment and aversion, enabling us to find tranquility within the ever-changing tides of life.

Perception plays a pivotal role in shaping our version of reality. The way our minds interpret the external world can dramatically reshape the texture of our experiences. Imagine donning a pair of lenses with vivid hues; suddenly, the world appears flushed with colors that shape the flavor of every interaction. Mindfulness practices are there to guide us in untangling these perceptual biases. By cultivating the skill of observing our thoughts and emotions without the weight of judgment, we can begin to discern how they morph our understanding of reality. This newly gained awareness empowers us to challenge preconceived notions and open ourselves to novel perspectives, much like a wave shifting the landscape of a sandy shore.

Explorations at the convergence of philosophy and mysticism yield fertile soil for delving into these profound ideas. Phenomenology, a philosophical branch dedicated to unraveling the fabric of subjective experience, resonates closely with the insights of mysticism. It implores us to peel back the layers of our experiences without the interference of settled assumptions, mirroring the profound journey of a mystic immersed in meditation or contemplation. This philosophical approach encourages us to perceive reality as a beautifully malleable entity, defined not by concreteness but by the sway of our perceptions and interpretations.

Mystical experiences, with their transformative power, can dramatically shift the contours of our understanding of reality. Often encompassing altered states of consciousness, these occurrences dissolve the boundaries separating self from other, cascading into a sensation of unity. Such experiences can offer fleeting glimpses into a realm that feels vastly inclusive and interconnected, going beyond the reach of our conventional awareness. See yourself in a lush forest, bathed in an inexplicable sense of unity with every tree, rustling leaf, and gentle breath of the wind. These rare moments can shift your entire worldview, prompting reconsideration of all you once held as definitive.

These profound insights extend a compelling invitation to embrace life through a lens far removed from the mundane. They remind us that reality is not merely a reflection of our superficial perceptions but rather a profound and intricate tapestry. Embracing these perspectives allows us entrance into a world filled with richer details and more nuanced meanings.

It becomes evident that delving into the nature of reality is not merely an intellectual pursuit but an invitation to perceive with a rejuvenated vision. Mystical philosophies invite us into the realm of questioning our long-held assumptions and embracing the transformative power of uncertainty as a portal to hidden truths, offering a pathway toward wisdom and freedom.

Next, we will explore practical methodologies for integrating these insights into the fabric of everyday life. This endeavor aims to equip you to balance the thirst for spiritual exploration with the commitments of daily duties. This passage is at once profoundly personal and intrinsically universal, allowing us to connect with the infinite while remaining grounded in daily reality.

Chapter Nine

Vivid Descriptions of Mystical States

The Bliss of Samadhi to Attain Unity with the Divine

You're in a tranquil garden, where time stands still, and everything resonates with a serene harmony. This is the profound peace of Samadhi, a state where the mind effortlessly finds stillness. In this silence, you feel cradled by the universe, every breath gently guided by an unseen force. The air is different here, thick with tranquility, wrapping around you like a soft cocoon. Your thoughts, usually restless, settle gently, allowing you to immerse yourself in a profound quietude that envelops your entire being.

Within this stillness, a radiant light begins to dawn from within, casting away shadows of doubt and fear. It's as though an inner sun has risen, illuminating not just your mind but your very soul. This isn't just a visual phenomenon; it's a deep-seated understanding that transcends ordinary perception. The light is warm and nurturing, and it spreads through every fiber of your being. In this space, you're not just observing the light—you become it. It's as if you've been living in grayscale, and suddenly, everything blooms into vivid colors. This inner illumination brings with it undeniable clarity and peace.

Emotionally, Samadhi unfolds like a tapestry of boundless love. You feel embraced by the universe itself, an embrace that offers unconditional acceptance and warmth. It's like being held by a loving parent after a long day—comforting and reassuring. This connection isn't limited to just the self; it extends outward, enveloping all of existence. The feeling is overwhelming yet serene, as if love itself were a tangible entity wrapping you in its gentle arms. Alongside this love is an infinite joy, a happiness that knows no bounds. It's the kind of joy that bubbles up from deep within, flowing through you like a river of pure delight.

Alongside this love is an infinite joy, a happiness that knows no bounds. It's the kind of joy that bubbles up from deep within, flowing through you like a river of pure delight. This isn't the fleeting happiness of material success or temporary pleasure; it's an enduring ecstasy that fills every nook and cranny of your consciousness. It transcends understanding or explanation, leaving only a profound sense of contentment in its wake.

As you journey deeper into Samadhi, your identity begins to dissolve like mist in the morning sun. The boundaries that once defined where "you" ended and "the world" began to fade into oblivion. It's not a loss but a liberation—a freeing from the constraints of ego that so often dictate thought and action. Here, there's no longer a need to protect or defend the self because you recognize there's nothing to defend against. You merge seamlessly with the divine essence that permeates all things.

The impact of Samadhi lingers long after the experience itself has faded. It reshapes perspectives and priorities in ways both subtle and profound. Suddenly, everyday concerns seem less pressing, dwarfed by the realization of interconnectedness with all life. This shift in consciousness fosters greater compassion and empathy, allowing for deeper connections with others. Material pursuits lose their luster as new values emerge centered around love, understanding, and spiritual growth. This enduring impact of Samadhi inspires and transforms, guiding you on a path of spiritual growth and understanding.

Embracing Samadhi's Gifts

- **Reflect on Moments of Inner Stillness:** Recall times when you felt completely at peace and connected with the world around you.

- **Explore Practices That Cultivate Samadhi:** Consider incorporating meditation or mindfulness exercises into your daily routine to cultivate this state of mind.

- **Journal About Your Experiences:** Write about how these practices influence your awareness and understanding of unity with the divine.

This glimpse into Samadhi offers a taste of what it means to transcend ordinary consciousness and touch the divine presence within us all.

Entering the Shamanic Trance for a Journey Within

In a dimly lit room, you sit, where the air is thick with anticipation, and the smell of sage lingers. As the rhythmic drumming begins, the sound is like a heartbeat coaxing you into another world. The pulsating beats echo through your body, each thud syncing with your pulse. It feels ancient, as if the drum carries the wisdom of centuries within its rhythm. Your mind starts to drift, following the beat like a boat on a gentle river, slowly leaving the shores of ordinary consciousness behind. The drumming becomes your anchor, guiding you deeper into a trance where reality begins to blur and a new realm unfurls before you.

In this altered state, visions of spirit animals start to appear, vivid and surreal. A wise old owl might swoop down to whisper secrets of the night, or a powerful wolf may walk beside you, offering strength and companionship. These aren't mere figments of imagination; they feel real, imbued with a presence that defies explanation. Each encounter carries its message, conveyed not in words but in feelings and images. These spirit animals often serve as guides, helping you navigate the symbolic landscapes that unfold in this mystical realm.

As you journey further into this state, landscapes that defy logic and gravity stretch out before you. You find yourself standing at the base of a sacred mountain, its peak shrouded in mist and mystery. Climbing symbolizes facing challenges and uncovering revelations about yourself and your path. It's both daunting and exhilarating, with each step bringing you closer to understanding hidden truths. Nearby, a river flows with a gentle yet insistent current, representing life's journey with all its twists and turns. The water sparkles under an ethereal light, inviting reflection on how life ebbs and flows, carrying joys and sorrows alike.

Amidst these landscapes, emotions swell and crest like waves against a shore. There's a profound release of fear as you confront inner demons in this safe space, allowing you to face shadows that linger just beyond waking life. It's not easy; confronting fears rarely is. Yet, here, in the heart of the trance, there is a sense of safety and support that enables vulnerability without judgment. This release is cathartic, leaving you lighter and more receptive to the insights that are waiting to emerge from within.

And then comes the moment of profound insight—a sudden clarity that cuts through confusion like sunlight piercing storm clouds. It's as if a puzzle piece clicks into place within your soul. You now understand aspects of your life's path that previously eluded you. These insights aren't always grand or earth-shattering; sometimes, they're simple truths that resonate deeply because they echo what you've always known but couldn't quite articulate. In these moments, everything falls into place in a way that is hard to describe, yet impossible to deny.

Once you return from this trance state, integrating these experiences into daily life becomes an ongoing process. It's not about clinging to visions or trying to recreate the trance; instead, it's about carrying its essence with you into everyday moments. Ritual tools, such as feathers or stones, can serve as tangible reminders of your inner journey. They act as anchors, helping you reconnect with the insights gained during your trance whenever needed.

Bringing these experiences into conscious awareness requires intention and a willingness to be patient. It involves reflecting on what you've learned and finding ways to apply those lessons in practical situations. It could be adopting new habits that align with your understanding or letting go of patterns that no longer serve you. The goal is to integrate these insights into your life. Hence, they become an integral part of who you are rather than distant memories.

This process isn't linear; it ebbs and flows like any journey worth taking. There will be times when integration feels effortless and others when it feels like an uphill climb. That's okay—each step brings growth and transformation in its way.

Incorporating these trance experiences into everyday life doesn't mean living perpetually in another realm; it means drawing strength from what you've discovered there to navigate this world with greater wisdom and resilience. Whether through meditation, creative expression, or simply being mindful throughout your day, let these insights be your guide as you continue to explore both inner landscapes and outer realities alike.

This glimpse into the shamanic trance offers a window into an extraordinary state where boundaries blur between self-awareness and spiritual exploration, where profound insights await those willing to listen beyond words alone.

The Luminous Void to Embrace the Unknown

You feel yourself floating in a seemingly endless, boundless expanse where the traditional parameters of reality start to dissolve gently, much like mist before the morning sun. This is the luminous void—a paradoxical state, if you will, where what appears to be emptiness is teeming with potential and vibrant awareness that seems nearly palpable. You find yourself in this infinite, formless expanse, much like a cosmic canvas, unmarked by preconceived notions or the weight of expectations. It's as though you've stepped into an ethereal realm where everything and nothing find a harmonious coexistence in a simultaneous symphony. The quiet fullness of this experience can be absolutely astounding, defying conventional understandings of what emptiness means, all the while filling you with a profound sense of presence and latent potential. Here, the absence of form signifies not a void but rather an expansive, limitless realm of possibilities eagerly waiting to unfold and reveal their mysteries.

As you drift into this space, emotionally entering the void induces a release quite unlike any other you have ever encountered. There is a profound sense of surrender to the vast emptiness, an intentional letting go of all attachments and expectations that bind you to the known and the comfortable. This act isn't one of passive resignation but rather an active embrace of what is. Imagine standing at the edge of a vast, unfathomable ocean, willingly stepping into its limitless depths with a trusting heart, without the fear of drowning. In this state, a surprising peace emerges amidst the uncertainty, the comfort found in the allure of the unknown and the softly undefined. You realize, in a moment of clarity, that not every question demands an immediate answer, nor does every problem insist upon having a solution. Sometimes, the most profound insights arise from simply being present in the mystery, allowing the experience to unfold naturally and reveal its wisdom.

Encountering the void can indeed be transformative in ways that are difficult to articulate. Emerging from such an experience often feels like a rebirth from emptiness, with new perspectives rising to replace old, outdated paradigms. The void strips away superficial layers like a gentle breeze, revealing the more profound truths about yourself and your place within the grand scheme of the universe. Personal growth becomes not just probable but inevitable as you reevaluate your priorities and reshape your understanding of what truly holds value and significance. This is not about acquiring something tangible but about discovering the richness that dwells within when everything else has been set aside gracefully.

Attempting to articulate the experience of the void presents a unique challenge. It dwells beyond the conventional confines of language, inhabiting a realm where words falter, stumbling and fumbling as if caught unprepared for the task at hand. The ineffability of the experience becomes apparent when you endeavor to convey it to others, only to find that language lacks the nuance and subtlety required to capture its whole essence. It's like trying to describe the color blue to someone who has never encountered it—impossible yet deeply, profoundly felt. This inability to fully express the void's impact does not diminish its power; instead, it highlights its profound, intimate nature, a silent reminder of its depth and majesty.

Despite these challenges, encountering the luminous void leaves an indelible mark on those who are brave enough to answer its call. It requires courage, not the obvious valor seen in tales of heroism, but understated bravery and curiosity, asking you to step beyond the familiar and into a space where possibilities are limitless, and dreams are given wings. In this mysterious realm, you're invited to explore not just the vast outer reaches of consciousness but also the rich inner depths rarely touched by ordinary awareness. This exploration isn't about drawing conclusions or finding definitive answers; it's about experiencing life in its most genuine form, unencumbered by expectation or definition.

The luminous void stands as a gentle reminder that actual growth often arises from moments of surrender rather than control. It offers an invitation to trust unabashedly in the unknown, to find peace amidst uncertainty, and to embrace the potential that lies within emptiness itself. As you navigate this uncharted territory, remember that you do not travel alone; numerous others have ventured into these depths before you, each returning with unique insights and newfound clarity.

Ultimately, the luminous void offers a glimpse into a world where boundaries blur and possibilities abound—a transcendent place where you can find solace in the unknown and discover astonishing beauty in emptiness. Here, you learn that, at times, the most meaningful experiences defy explanation, existing beyond the realm of words and yet resonating deeply within the core of your soul, beckoning you towards a deeper understanding of the infinite mysteries of existence.

The Mystical Ecstasy of Oneness

Imagine a moment when the universe seems to hum in perfect harmony around you. It's as if every cell in your body vibrates in sync with the cosmos, creating a sensation of vibrational harmony that draws you into a profound state of unity. This isn't just a fleeting feeling; it's an all-encompassing experience, like being enveloped in a warm, embracing presence from the universe itself. You find yourself dissolving into an oceanic bliss, where boundaries cease to exist and your essence mingles with the infinite whole. It's like standing at the edge of a vast ocean, each wave a part of you, carrying you into the depths of cosmic unity.

In this ecstatic experience, the dissolution of duality becomes vividly apparent. Here, the lines that once separated you from the world around you blur into nonexistence. You perceive yourself as one with all life, nature, humanity, and even the stars above. It's as if the world breathes as one organism, and you are an integral part of its rhythm. This unity with all life fosters an understanding that transcends words, an innate recognition of interconnectedness that defies ordinary logic. You realize that every breath you take is shared with every being, echoing through the tapestry of existence.

The emotional intensity of oneness is overwhelming. It's a transcendent joy that sweeps you off your feet, lifting you into realms where ordinary emotions seem pale by comparison. This euphoria fills every corner of your being, radiating outward in waves of happiness that know no bounds. It feels like a celebration of life itself—a dance with a creation that leaves you breathless and exhilarated. Accompanying this joy is a universal love, an affection so profound it envelops everything it touches. It's an all-encompassing embrace, reaching out to every creature and every element of existence with unreserved warmth and kindness.

Experiencing oneness leaves a lasting imprint on your worldview and behavior. Suddenly, life takes on new meaning as compassion and empathy become guiding principles. The understanding that all beings are interconnected encourages a compassionate living mindset—acting from a place of empathy and shared humanity. You find yourself more attuned to the needs of others, recognizing their struggles as reflections of your own. This newfound awareness transforms interactions, fostering kindness and understanding even in the most mundane exchanges.

The shift in perspective brought about by oneness extends beyond interpersonal relationships, permeating every aspect of life. Material pursuits lose their allure as you prioritize connection and growth over the accumulation of things. The desire for personal gain gives way to a longing for collective well-being, and decisions are made with consideration for how they impact not just you but the world at large. This transformation isn't forced or contrived; it flows naturally from the realization that you are part of something far greater than yourself.

Oneness invites you to explore what it truly means to be alive—to experience life not as an isolated individual but as an integral part of a vibrant whole. It encourages you to see beauty in diversity and strength in unity, cultivating a sense of belonging that transcends borders and boundaries. As you navigate this new way of being, remember that each step toward unity brings with it opportunities for growth and transformation.

This chapter has explored various mystical states—Samadhi's blissful peace, shamanic trances' introspective journeys, the luminous void's boundless potential, and cosmic unity's ecstatic embrace—all of which offer unique insights into the nature of consciousness and existence. Each state provides glimpses into realms where ordinary perceptions are expanded beyond measure, revealing truths that resonate deeply within our souls.

As we move forward into the next chapter, we'll continue to unravel these mysteries by examining how ancient wisdom can inform modern practices—integrating timeless teachings into our everyday lives for greater fulfillment and understanding. Let us continue this exploration with open hearts and curious minds, ever ready to embrace the unknown with courage and grace.

Chapter Ten

The Transformative Power of Mysticism

Mysticism as a Path to Inner Peace

You're sitting by a gentle stream, the water's lullaby soothing your mind, washing away the weight of the world. This natural tranquility is akin to the peace mysticism offers. Through its practices, mysticism cultivates a profound sense of inner calm. By engaging with these practices, you can create an oasis of serenity amidst life's relentless chaos.

Silent retreats offer a unique opportunity to delve deep within yourself, creating a space for introspection that's often hard to find in daily life. In these retreats, where words are stilled, you can hear your inner voice more clearly. The silence strips away distractions, allowing you to confront your thoughts and emotions head-on. These retreats become a sanctuary for personal growth and reflection, where peace seeps into your very being (6 Powerful Benefits Of Silent Retreats, n.d.).

Mindfulness in nature provides another avenue to access inner tranquility. Walking through a forest or sitting by the ocean immerses you in the present moment. Nature's rhythms slow your heartbeat, grounding you in a simple truth: you are part of something greater. This connection fosters a serene state where stress melts away, leaving room for peace and a profound sense of calm.

The impact of inner peace on daily living is profound. When you cultivate calm through mystical practices, stress reduction becomes a natural byproduct. Anxiety loses its grip, leaving you more resilient in the face of life's challenges. A tranquil mind enhances emotional resilience, enabling you to navigate life's storms with greater poise and grace.

Improved relationships are another benefit of achieving inner peace. When you approach interactions from a place of calm, you foster harmony and understanding. Communication becomes more meaningful as you listen with empathy and respond with compassion. This fosters stronger connections and deepens bonds with those around you.

Integrating these practices into daily life can be simple yet transformative. Daily meditation rituals anchor your day, providing a moment of quiet reflection amid the noise. Set aside time each morning or evening to sit in silence, focusing on your breath or a mantra. This routine centers you, nurturing peace within.

Gratitude practices further cultivate an attitude of appreciation, shifting the focus from what is lacking to what is present. By acknowledging small blessings each day, you invite positivity and contentment into your life. A gratitude journal or simple mental note can remind you of life's beauty and abundance, fostering a sense of appreciation and positivity.

Maintaining inner peace in a chaotic world presents significant challenges. The modern world bombards us with distractions and stressors that make tranquility elusive. Mindful detachment becomes essential in managing these external influences. By observing distractions without attachment, you maintain control over your inner state, empowering you to stay calm and in control amidst the chaos.

Emotional awareness is crucial for navigating inner turmoil with self-compassion. Recognizing and accepting emotions without judgment allows you to process them healthily. Self-compassion nurtures resilience, enabling you to face life's ups and downs with kindness and understanding.

Cultivating Inner Peace

- **Daily Reflection:** Set aside 5-10 minutes daily for quiet reflection. Focus on your breath, allowing thoughts to pass without engaging with them.

- **G.L.A.D. Technique:** Each evening, write down and reflect on these moments to foster appreciation and positivity.

  - **G - GRATITUDE:** What are you grateful for today, sunny weather, life, your child, a test result?

  - **L - LEARNED:** What is new to you, something about yourself, added knowledge, something you didn't know yesterday?

  - **A - ACCOMPLISHMENT:** What did you achieve today, you finished task, made someone happy?

  - **D - DELIGHT:** What is something that gave you great pleasure, made you laugh or smile?

- **Mindful Nature Walk:** Spend time in nature weekly, observing its beauty and feeling a sense of connection to its rhythms.

By incorporating these practices into your life, you can cultivate inner peace amid chaos. Mysticism provides tools for serenity and growth, transforming your engagement with the world around you.

Awakening to Your True Self

Mysticism beckons you to discover your authentic self, a concept as exhilarating as it is transformative. At the heart of this exploration lies the Higher Self—a part of you that transcends the limitations of the ego. This essence isn't swayed by external validation or fleeting emotions; instead, it resonates with a more profound truth, one that aligns with your spiritual identity and place in the universe. Mysticism encourages you to peel back layers of societal expectations and personal fears, revealing a purer understanding of who you are. It's about acknowledging the vastness within, recognizing that you're more than the roles you play or the labels you've been given.

Embracing your true self often begins with introspective journaling. This practice invites you to explore your beliefs and desires, offering a mirror to reflect on what truly matters to you. As you write, consider these questions: What are your core values? What do you truly want from life? Journaling allows you to sift through thoughts and emotions, discarding those that don't serve your highest good. It becomes a sanctuary for honesty and clarity, guiding you closer to your true essence.

Guided visualizations offer another powerful tool for self-discovery. By imagining your ideal self and life, you step into possibilities beyond current limitations. Picture yourself living fully, free of societal constraints—what does that look like? Feel like? These visualizations help bridge the gap between who you are and who you're meant to be. They serve as a roadmap, guiding your thoughts and actions toward authenticity.

Recognizing your authentic self brings transformative power. As self-awareness blossoms, so does confidence. Knowing who you are at your core empowers you to navigate life with assurance. Decisions become clearer, motivated by inner truth rather than external pressures. This newfound confidence is contagious, influencing how you interact with the world and inviting opportunities aligned with your authentic self.

Living authentically means that actions and values align seamlessly. It's about walking your talk and expressing your truth in every interaction. Authentic living requires courage—courage to stand firm in your beliefs even when they contradict societal norms or expectations. It involves embracing vulnerabilities as strengths and acknowledging imperfections as part of the whole. This alignment fosters a life rich with purpose and fulfillment, where each day resonates with meaning.

To nurture self-awareness and authenticity, practical exercises can be invaluable. Reflective meditation offers moments of focused contemplation on personal truth. Set aside time regularly to sit quietly and ask yourself: What truths am I living? Where do I compromise my values? This practice encourages honesty and insight, fostering deeper connections with oneself.

Value identification is another essential exercise in this process. By recognizing and prioritizing core principles, you develop a compass to guide decisions and actions. Consider listing the values most important to you—such as integrity, compassion, and creativity—and reflect on how they manifest in your daily life. Are there areas needing realignment? This awareness strengthens resolve, ensuring choices reflect true intentions.

Navigating this path isn't always easy. The world often demands conformity, challenging authenticity at every turn. But by embracing these practices, you fortify resilience against external pressures. You learn to trust intuition over noise, cultivating a life aligned with your true self.

Mysticism whispers that within lies vast potential waiting to be realized—that beneath layers of ego and expectation rests an essence yearning for expression. This journey towards authenticity transforms not only individual lives but ripples outward, touching all encountered along the way.

Your true self isn't something to be found; it's something to be remembered, nurtured back into existence through mindful practices and courageous choices. In awakening to this truth lies liberation—freedom that allows you not just to exist but to thrive authentically amidst life's complexities.

Embracing Change through Mystical Practice

Life, with its constant ebb and flow, often demands we adapt. Mysticism offers a unique perspective on navigating these transitions. It teaches us that change isn't something to fear but to embrace. By cultivating spiritual resilience, you build the strength to adapt to life's ever-shifting landscape. Think of it as developing a mental and spiritual toolkit that helps you face new circumstances with an open heart and mind. This resilience doesn't come from avoiding change but from diving into it headfirst, confident that you have the inner resources to handle whatever comes your way.

Acceptance and surrender are central to this process. Often, we resist change because we fear the unknown or cling to the familiar. Mysticism encourages letting go of this resistance. It's about acknowledging that not everything is within our control and finding peace in that realization. By surrendering to the natural flow of life, you can release anxiety and welcome change as a catalyst for growth. This doesn't mean passively accepting everything that happens, but instead choosing to respond with wisdom and insight.

Incorporating mystical practices into your life can help you navigate transitions with greater ease and grace. Visualization is a powerful tool for embracing change. By envisioning positive outcomes, you create a mental map of what you want to achieve. Picture yourself thriving amidst change, adapting like a river flowing around obstacles. This mental imagery helps align your thoughts and actions with your desired reality, making change feel less daunting and more manageable.

Affirmation practices reinforce adaptability and openness. By repeating affirmations like "I welcome change and grow through it" or "Every transition brings new opportunities," you can rewire your brain to view change in a more positive light. These affirmations become a mantra, guiding you through turbulent times with a steady hand.

Embracing change also offers rich growth opportunities—viewing challenges as stepping stones instead of roadblocks can transform your perspective. Every obstacle contains lessons waiting to be uncovered. It's about shifting from a mindset of fear to one of curiosity, asking yourself what this change can teach you. This approach transforms challenges into opportunities for learning and personal development.

Expanding your horizons is another gift of embracing change. New experiences push you out of your comfort zone, broadening your perspectives and enriching your life. By stepping into unfamiliar territory, you discover strengths and capabilities you never knew existed. This expansion isn't just about external experiences; it's about internal growth—the kind that deepens understanding and fosters compassion.

Consider the story of Jane, who faced an unexpected career change after two decades in the same job. Initially, she struggled with fear and uncertainty. However, by engaging in mystical practices such as journaling and meditation, she began to see this transition as an opportunity for reinvention. Through visualization exercises, she envisioned herself succeeding in a new field that aligned with her passions. Her affirmations reinforced her belief in her adaptability. Today, Jane thrives in her new career, grateful for the growth that came from embracing change.

Another example is Michael, who experienced a challenging personal transition after a significant relationship ended. Instead of dwelling on loss, he turned to mysticism for guidance. Through reflective meditation, Michael found acceptance and inner peace. He learned to appreciate the lessons from his past while remaining open to future possibilities. This shift allowed him to embark on new adventures with confidence and optimism.

These stories highlight the transformative power of embracing change through mystical practice. Change isn't something to dread but to welcome as an opportunity for growth and discovery. Mysticism provides tools that help navigate life's transitions with grace—tools that foster resilience, acceptance, and personal development.

As life continues its unpredictable dance, remember that each step offers an invitation to grow stronger and wiser. By using mystical practices as a guide, you can learn not only to survive but thrive amidst life's inevitable changes. Through acceptance, visualization, and affirmation, you harness the power of transformation within yourself, creating a life rich in purpose, meaning, and endless growth potential.

Engage with these practices wholeheartedly; let them become part of your daily routine. Allow them to shape your perspective on change—transforming fear into excitement, resistance into acceptance—and watch as they open doors previously unseen.

The Alchemy of Personal Transformation

Alchemy, in its mystical sense, isn't about turning lead into gold. It's about transforming the self, taking the raw, unrefined parts of who you are, and turning them into something truly valuable. Think of it as a metaphor for personal change, where you harness the challenges and trials of life to create your version of the Philosopher's Stone—achieving spiritual enlightenment. This transformation involves recognizing personal challenges as opportunities for growth, much like alchemists saw potential in base metals. By facing these challenges head-on, you transform weaknesses into strengths, gaining wisdom and resilience in the process.

The stages of alchemical transformation mirror those of personal growth. The first stage, calcination, involves burning away the false self. Here, you confront and release limiting beliefs and outdated habits that no longer serve you. It's a process of purification and letting go, stripping away layers to reveal your true essence. This stage might feel intense, as it involves confronting uncomfortable truths about yourself. But it's necessary for growth, creating space for new insights to emerge.

Coagulation follows as the next stage, where you solidify these newfound insights and growth. Here, the transformation becomes tangible as you integrate lessons learned into your daily life. It's about taking the wisdom gained from calcination and using it to shape your reality. This stage involves committing to new habits and mindsets that align with your authentic self. Through coagulation, you begin to see the results of your efforts as your inner world shifts to reflect your evolving identity.

Challenges and trials play a crucial role in this transformation process. They are the alchemical crucible in which personal growth occurs. Each obstacle you face acts as a catalyst for change, pushing you to expand and adapt. Embracing trials with courage and curiosity allows you to extract valuable lessons from them. These challenges aren't meant to break you but to refine you, much like fire refines gold. By viewing obstacles as opportunities for growth, you shift your perspective from one of fear to one of empowerment.

To engage in this alchemical process of transformation, consider incorporating symbolic rituals into your life. These rituals mark stages of transformation, providing structure and meaning to your journey. Whether it's a simple candle lighting to signify release or a more elaborate ceremony to celebrate milestones, rituals create a sacred space for reflection and intention-setting. They serve as reminders of your commitment to personal growth and transformation.

Reflective practice is another crucial element in this process. Continuously assessing your progress and adapting as needed ensures that you remain aligned with your goals. This involves regular self-assessment, where you honestly evaluate your thoughts, actions, and beliefs. Ask yourself: Are my actions reflecting my values? Am I making progress toward the transformation I desire? This ongoing reflection keeps you accountable and ensures that you stay on track.

The beauty of alchemy lies in its reminder that transformation is an ongoing process. There is no final destination or point of completion. Instead, it's about embracing the journey of constant evolution—recognizing that each stage builds upon the last, leading to greater self-awareness and enlightenment.

Remember that change is not only possible but also inevitable when approached with intention and openness. The journey may be challenging at times, but it's also incredibly gratifying. By engaging in this process with courage and curiosity, you unlock your potential for growth and self-discovery.

In the next chapter, we'll explore how mystical practices can deepen our understanding of interconnectedness and unity with all things. This exploration will further illuminate the path toward personal transformation by expanding our awareness beyond individual experiences toward a collective consciousness that unites us all.

Chapter Eleven

Mysticism in the Modern World

Mysticism in the Digital Age Offers Opportunities and Challenges

Imagine for a moment that the entire world's mystical knowledge is like an expansive library, and now, thanks to the digital age, you hold the keys to it. With just a few clicks, you can access teachings from countless mystical traditions. This unprecedented access empowers you, offering a modern classroom where seekers gather across continents, share insights, and discover new perspectives together. Virtual meditation apps are your pocket-sized guides, providing tools for mindfulness practices whenever you need a moment of calm. However, this incredible access also brings its own set of hurdles.

The constant buzz of notifications can yank your focus away from deep spiritual engagement. Social media overload is a beast, bombarding you with endless streams of information, some enriching, while others are less so. That's where the concept of a digital detox comes into play.

Unplugging from the digital world, even briefly, can restore your spiritual clarity. It's a chance to pause, reflect, and connect with your inner self, free from digital noise. This intentional disconnection helps foster a more meaningful connection when you engage with technology.

Despite these challenges, digital platforms offer immense benefits for spiritual communities. Online forums and groups have become sanctuaries for seekers who crave connection and support. These virtual spaces offer a sense of belonging, providing opportunities to discuss experiences and share wisdom and creating virtual circles that nurture personal growth. Virtual retreats provide immersive experiences that enable you to delve deeply into spiritual practices from the comfort of your own home, eliminating the need for travel. These digital communities form bonds that transcend physical distance, uniting kindred spirits in shared exploration.

To navigate this digital landscape mindfully, it's crucial to find balance. Set boundaries for your technology use and prioritize quality over quantity in your digital interactions. This balanced approach ensures that your online presence complements, rather than detracts from, your spiritual practice, providing you with a sense of control and reassurance in the digital age.

Mindful Tech Use Checklist

- **Set Daily Tech Limits:** Decide how much time you'll spend online each day.

- **Designate Tech-Free Zones:** Create designated areas where the use of technology is prohibited.

- **Schedule Regular Digital Detoxes:** Plan times to disconnect entirely.

- **Engage with Purpose:** Choose online activities that align with your spiritual goals.

- **Reflect on Your Digital Habits:** Regularly assess how technology affects your well-being.

By integrating these strategies, you can harness the benefits of technology while safeguarding your spiritual journey from digital distractions. The digital age offers unprecedented opportunities to explore mysticism, but it requires mindful engagement to truly reap its rewards.

Environmental Mysticism to Connect with Nature

See yourself standing in a lush forest where sunlight filters through the leaves, casting dappled shadows on the ground. Nature isn't just a backdrop; it mirrors your inner state, reflecting emotions and thoughts. This concept of environmental mysticism underscores the profound spiritual insights that the natural world offers. Sacred groves, revered historically, symbolize places where nature and spirit intertwine. These spaces remind us that nature has long been a conduit for mystical experiences, serving as a mirror for our souls.

In exploring the Gaia Hypothesis, we encounter the idea that Earth functions as a living organism. This perspective aligns beautifully with mystical principles, emphasizing interconnectedness and unity. Seeing Earth as a singular entity fosters a deeper ecological consciousness, encouraging us to recognize our role within this vast, living system. This approach shifts our perception from one of dominion over nature to one of partnership, thereby enhancing our spiritual connection to the planet.

To deepen your connection with nature, consider practices such as forest bathing and nature meditation. Forest bathing, originating in Japan, involves immersing yourself in a natural setting, allowing the sights, sounds, and smells to soothe your spirit. This practice isn't about hiking or exercising; it's about being present with nature's rhythms. Similarly, nature meditation invites mindfulness in outdoor spaces, encouraging you to observe and engage with the environment reflectively. These practices ground you, fostering a sense of peace and a deeper sense of belonging.

Environmental mysticism not only nurtures personal growth but also inspires sustainable living. By integrating eco-spirituality into your practice, you cultivate an awareness that influences everyday choices. This mindset encourages mindful consumption and respect for all living things, promoting sustainability. As you become more attuned to nature's cycles, you naturally adopt habits that support ecological balance. This shift in consciousness not only enhances personal well-being but also contributes to collective environmental stewardship.

The journey toward environmental mysticism involves embracing nature as both a teacher and partner. You learn to listen to the whispers of the wind and the stories told by ancient trees, finding wisdom in their presence. This connection fosters a deeper appreciation for the world around you, encouraging you to live in harmony with all life forms. Through this lens, every walk in the park becomes a sacred pilgrimage, each breath a reminder of your bond with the Earth.

A New Paradigm for Mysticism and Social Change

Consider a world where mystical principles inspire movements for change and where spirituality fuels the drive for social activism. The core of nonviolent resistance lies in its spiritual foundations. Figures like Gandhi and Martin Luther King Jr. drew from deep reservoirs of spiritual wisdom to champion peaceful protest. Their leadership, rooted in empathy and understanding, showcased compassionate leadership in action. It's not just about strategy; it's a way of being. This approach challenges us to lead with love, seeing beyond differences and fostering unity.

At the intersection of mysticism and social justice, spiritual values promote equality and fairness. Spiritual activism merges practice with action, urging us to bring our insights into the world. It's about aligning inner peace with outer change. The teachings that guide personal growth can also guide societies toward justice. When we practice mindfulness or meditation, we cultivate patience and empathy—qualities essential for transformative social action.

Mystical experiences have the power to catalyze societal transformation. Personal awakenings ripple outward, inspiring collective change. Unity consciousness becomes more than an idea; it's a lived experience fostering global interconnectedness. As individuals awaken to their true nature, they naturally extend compassion to others, creating a web of positive influence that touches countless lives. This collective awakening encourages communities to work together toward shared goals, breaking down the barriers that divide them.

Several initiatives beautifully integrate mysticism with social change. Movements driven by spirituality often emphasize peace and understanding. These peaceful movements stand as testaments to the power of spirituality-driven activism. Organizations worldwide harness the transformative power of mystical experiences to foster dialogue and reconciliation. By focusing on common humanity rather than differences, they create spaces for healing and growth.

Consider the example of a community that organizes meditation retreats alongside social justice workshops. Participants engage in deep self-reflection as they learn about the systemic issues that affect marginalized groups. This unique blend of introspection and education empowers individuals to make informed contributions to social change efforts. By incorporating both inner exploration and external action, these initiatives embody a holistic approach to transformation.

In this evolving landscape, mysticism offers a new paradigm for societal progress. It invites us to envision a world where compassion leads, unity thrives, and justice prevails through spiritual insights woven into the fabric of our lives.

The Future of Mysticism for Bridging Tradition and Innovation

Now, you're standing at a crossroads where ancient wisdom meets modern insight. This intersection is rich with potential, creating new paradigms by blending traditional teachings with contemporary knowledge. Cross-cultural syncretism emerges when elements from diverse mystical traditions merge, offering a tapestry of spiritual exploration. You might find practices that combine the meditative discipline of Zen with the ecstatic dance of Sufi whirling. Modern mystics act as bridges, drawing from the past to enrich the present landscape, showing how to adapt age-old wisdom to today's challenges.

Innovation plays a pivotal role in evolving mystical practices. New tools and methodologies enhance spiritual exploration, offering fresh avenues for insight and growth. Technological innovations like virtual reality provide immersive mystical experiences, transporting you to realms once accessible only through intense meditation or pilgrimage. Imagine slipping on a VR headset and finding yourself in a sacred temple or tranquil forest, engaging all your senses in a way that deepens your practice.

However, preserving tradition while embracing change presents challenges. It's vital to maintain authenticity when adapting practices, ensuring cultural respect by honoring the origins and context of mystical teachings. This balance requires sensitivity and awareness, recognizing when modern adaptations enhance the essence and when they risk diluting it.

Modern adaptations breathe new life into traditional practices. Mindfulness, once rooted in ancient meditation techniques, now appears in various forms tailored for contemporary life. Whether it's mindful eating or workplace meditation sessions, these adaptations make ancient wisdom accessible and relevant, helping you integrate spirituality into daily routines without losing its core.

The future of mysticism invites you to explore this dynamic dance between tradition and innovation. It encourages you to respect the roots while experimenting with new expressions. By doing so, you participate in a living tradition that continually evolves, bridging the past with the present. This blend of old and new offers a path rich with possibility, inviting you to engage with mysticism in ways that resonate deeply, both personally and collectively.

Crafting a Personal Mystical Path in Today's World

In our fast-paced world, personalizing your spiritual practice is not just beneficial but vital. Imagine weaving a tapestry that reflects your unique beliefs and lifestyle. Tailoring practices means adapting techniques to fit your individual needs, ensuring that your spiritual path resonates with who you truly are. This might mean starting your day with a simple meditation or ending it with gratitude journaling. Your path should bring you joy and peace, not feel like a chore. It's about creating a spiritual routine that aligns with your life, not one that feels forced or disconnected.

Listening to your intuition can be like having an internal compass guiding you through the fog of external opinions. Trusting personal insights over prescribed methods allows you to navigate your spiritual development with authenticity. Your inner voice often knows what's best for you, even when others might suggest otherwise. It's about finding what speaks to your soul, not just following the latest trend in spirituality. Intuition can lead you down paths you never expected, opening up new avenues for growth and understanding.

Crafting a personalized spiritual practice involves intentional goal-setting, defining what you want to achieve spiritually, and setting milestones to track your progress. This intentionality can help you stay focused and motivated. Incorporating diverse modalities—such as yoga, meditation, and nature walks—ensures a holistic approach, nurturing various aspects of your being. A balanced practice encompasses a variety of experiences, enriching your life beyond the confines of a single discipline. This variety keeps your spiritual life dynamic and engaging.

A self-directed mystical journey empowers you to take charge of your spiritual evolution. When you actively shape your path, the connection deepens, and growth feels more authentic. Empowerment comes from knowing you're steering your spiritual ship, not just riding along passively. Ownership of your practice fosters a sense of responsibility and commitment to your development. This self-guided approach encourages exploration and experimentation, allowing for continuous adaptation as you grow.

As you navigate this personal path, remember that there's no right or wrong way to explore spirituality. What matters is that it resonates with you and supports your growth. Embrace the freedom to try new things, discard what doesn't work, and refine what does. Your spiritual path should be as unique as you are, reflecting your ever-evolving understanding of self and the world around you. Each step on this path is an opportunity to learn more about yourself and deepen your connection with something greater.

A Community Approach to Engaging with Mysticism

Have you ever sat in a room filled with eager voices and shared stories, each tale weaving a tapestry of collective wisdom? This is the magic of community in spiritual growth. When you engage with others on a similar path, you tap into a reservoir of diverse experiences and insights. Learning from others enriches your understanding, providing perspectives you may not have considered. It's like a potluck where everyone brings a dish, and you get to feast on a variety of flavors, each one expanding your palate.

Communities don't just offer wisdom; they provide emotional support. Being part of a network means having people who encourage you when you're struggling and celebrate with you when you achieve breakthroughs. These connections create accountability, gently nudging you to stay committed to your spiritual practices. It's much easier to maintain momentum when you're not going it alone, knowing there's a safety net ready to catch you if you falter.

Modern mystical communities are evolving to meet the needs of contemporary society. Local meetups and circles provide spaces for in-person gatherings, where shared practices foster bonds that deepen over time. These connections aren't just about sharing meditation techniques or discussing mystical texts; they are about forming a deeper understanding of the world. They're about creating a supportive environment where everyone feels valued and heard. Open dialogue is crucial here, as it encourages diverse perspectives and fosters respectful conversations that promote growth and understanding. When everyone has a voice, the community becomes a living entity, constantly evolving and adapting to its surroundings.

The role of community in sustaining mystical engagement cannot be overstated. Shared rituals and celebrations bring people together, reinforcing their commitment to their spiritual paths. Whether it's celebrating the changing seasons or participating in group meditations, these activities create a rhythm that resonates with the cycles of life. They remind us that we're part of something larger, a collective consciousness that transcends individual experiences.

To foster an inclusive and supportive community, focus on creating a welcoming atmosphere. Encourage openness and empathy, ensuring that everyone feels comfortable sharing their thoughts and feelings. By nurturing these connections, you build a community that not only supports individual growth but also strengthens the collective spirit. This communal approach enriches your mystical engagement, making it more meaningful and fulfilling.

Mysticism's Role in Global Consciousness

Picture a world where mystical insights guide us toward global awareness, fostering a sense of interconnectedness that transcends borders. Mysticism has the potential to cultivate this oneness by nurturing connections beyond our immediate circles and encouraging empathy on a grand scale. As individuals awaken to their spiritual truths, they contribute to a collective consciousness that ripples outward, touching lives in both subtle and profound ways. Personal transformations can act as catalysts for broader societal shifts, inspiring others to explore their spiritual depths.

These individual awakenings create a ripple effect, like pebbles dropped into a calm pond. As one person embraces mysticism, their newfound clarity and compassion influence those around them, sparking curiosity and introspection in others. This domino effect can lead to significant cultural change as more people recognize the interconnected nature of all life. This awareness fosters a shared responsibility for the well-being of our planet and its inhabitants. When you realize that your actions have a ripple effect on the whole, you're more likely to act with kindness and consideration.

International conferences and events play a critical role in spreading mystical insights across cultures. These gatherings bring together voices from diverse backgrounds, fostering dialogue and understanding. They provide opportunities for cross-cultural exchange, where traditional wisdom intertwines with contemporary perspectives. Imagine the richness of conversations where ancient teachings meet modern challenges, offering solutions that honor both heritage and innovation. Such events inspire participants to carry newfound knowledge back to their communities, further amplifying the impact.

However, fostering global consciousness through mysticism also presents challenges and opportunities. Bridging cultural differences requires sensitivity and respect for varied traditions. It's about finding common ground while honoring unique paths. This delicate balance requires open-mindedness and a willingness to learn from one another. As we seek to unite diverse perspectives, we encounter both obstacles and opportunities for growth. The potential for unity lies in embracing our shared humanity while celebrating the diversity that enriches our world.

The journey toward global awareness through mysticism is one of mutual discovery and collaboration. It invites us to step outside our comfort zones and engage with perspectives that challenge our assumptions. By doing so, we contribute to a more conscious and connected world, where every individual's awakening enhances the collective understanding. This tapestry, woven with threads of insight and compassion, holds the power to transform not only ourselves but also the world we inhabit.

Everyday Practices for a Transformative Life and Living Mystically

Incorporating mystical practices into your daily routine can be a game-changer. It's about weaving small, consistent habits into your life that build up to something profound over time. Think of it like planting seeds that grow into a lush garden. Daily mindfulness is a powerful tool here. It's not just about sitting in meditation for hours; it's about being present in whatever you do. Whether you're washing dishes or walking to work, bringing your full attention to the moment transforms the mundane into something sacred.

Practical examples of living mystically are often simpler than you might think. Take gratitude journaling, for instance. By jotting down moments of appreciation each day, you shift your focus from what's lacking to what's abundant. This practice doesn't just lift your spirits; it rewires your brain to be more positive. Another accessible method is intentional breathing. Using your breath to center and ground yourself throughout the day can anchor you in times of chaos. Just a few deep breaths can clear your mind and reset your perspective.

Living a mystical life offers holistic benefits that ripple through every aspect of your existence. You'll likely find an enhanced quality of life marked by increased joy, peace, and satisfaction. It's like seeing an inner calm that weathers life's storms with grace. This doesn't mean you'll never face challenges, but your response to them transforms. You become more resilient and more connected to what truly matters.

The transformative potential of this lifestyle is immense. Sustained mystical engagement leads to lifelong growth, continuously evolving as you deepen your understanding and connection to the world around you. It's a journey of self-discovery and growth that continually unveils new layers of insight and wisdom. As you grow personally, you also contribute to collective transformation, inspiring others through your example.

In wrapping up this chapter, remember that integrating mystical practices into everyday life is like sprinkling magic into the ordinary. It doesn't require radical changes, just a gentle shift in awareness and intention. As we move forward, we'll explore how these practices can help deepen your connection with the divine and others, enriching both personal and communal experiences in ways you might not have imagined.

Conclusion

As we conclude our shared journey, I trust you now feel a profound sense of connection and understanding that was not as palpable at the beginning. We've traversed the intricate tapestry of mystical traditions, untangling the threads that bind ancient wisdom to our contemporary lives. From the historical origins of mysticism in early civilizations to the vibrant practices thriving today, we've explored diverse paths like Sufism, Zen, and Kabbalah. Each tradition offers unique insights, yet they all share a common quest for deeper truth and connection.

Throughout this book, my aim has been to blend history with practical guidance, demonstrating that mysticism is not reserved for scholars or sages. It is a powerful tool for anyone seeking to enrich their life with meaning and peace. We've examined the scientific perspectives that align with mystical experiences, bridging the gap between the tangible and the transcendent. By immersing in the vivid descriptions of mystical states, I hope you've been able to imagine and feel the profound experiences that mystics throughout history have described and realize that these experiences are within your reach.

The vision for this book was to challenge what we often take for granted. Mysticism invites us to look beyond the surface of everyday life. It asks us to question, reflect, and grow. The practices and exercises shared here are tools designed to help you cultivate inner peace and connect more deeply with the universe. Whether it's through meditation, visualization, or simply a moment of mindful breathing, these practices can transform the mundane into something extraordinary.

As you continue your journey, I encourage you to embrace the exercises and reflections we've discussed. Mysticism is a personal journey, and what resonates with you may be different from what resonates with someone else. Explore different traditions, follow your curiosity, and trust your intuition. Your path is uniquely yours, and there is no right or wrong way to walk it.

I also encourage you to seek out community. Sharing your journey with others can offer support, insight, and inspiration. Whether you join a local group or participate in an online forum, exchanging ideas and experiences can enrich your understanding and deepen your practice. The community offers a space for learning, sharing, and growth together.

Remember, the journey doesn't end here. Keep an open mind as you explore and reflect on your experiences. Consider keeping a journal to document your thoughts, questions, and insights. This can be a powerful tool for ongoing self-discovery and growth. Mysticism is not a destination but a lifelong exploration. It's about continually evolving and expanding your understanding of yourself and the world around you.

Looking forward, I envision a future where the wisdom of mystical traditions influences how we live and interact. Imagine a world where individuals and societies are more conscious, compassionate, and interconnected. The insights from this book are just the beginning. They inspire you to contribute to this vision in your own unique way.

Thank you for allowing me to be part of your journey. As you move forward, may you find peace, joy, and profound connection in every step you take. Stay curious, stay open, and embrace the mysticism that lies within and around you.

Glossary

- **Ajna Chakra** – The "Third Eye" chakra, linked to intuition, insight, and spiritual perception.

- **Alchemy** – A spiritual and proto-scientific tradition seeking the transformation of matter and self.

- **Animism** – Belief that all natural things possess a spiritual essence or consciousness.

- **Archetypes** – Universal symbols or themes found across cultures and in the collective unconscious.

- **Bhakti yoga** – A Hindu path of devotion and love directed toward a personal deity.

- **Buddhism** – A spiritual tradition centered on overcoming suffering through mindfulness and wisdom.

- **Celtic carvings** – Sacred symbols in stone, often representing nature, cycles, and mystical forces.

- **Christian monasticism** – A lifestyle of religious devotion through celibacy, prayer, and communal living.

- **Corpus Hermeticum** – A collection of mystical texts attributed to Hermes Trismegistus.

- **Dervishes** – Sufi ascetics known for spiritual practices, including whirling dances for divine union.

- **Dualism** – Belief in the separation of two fundamental principles, such as spirit and matter.

- **Eightfold Path in Buddhism** – Guiding principles to end suffering and attain enlightenment.

- **Ein Sof** – In Kabbalah, the infinite, unknowable aspect of God beyond all comprehension.

- **Eye of Horus** – Egyptian symbol of protection, healing, and spiritual insight.

- **Gaia Hypothesis** – Theory that Earth behaves as a self-regulating living organism.

- **Hermes Trismegistus** – Mythic figure symbolizing the fusion of Greek and Egyptian wisdom traditions.

- **Hermeticism** – A mystical philosophy focused on divine knowledge, alchemy, and cosmic unity.

- **Hindu chakra** – Energy centers in the subtle body that influence mind, body, and spirit.

- **Hindu Mysticism** – Spiritual practices in Hinduism aimed at union with the divine.

- **Ibn Arabi** – Influential Sufi mystic known for his concept of divine unity and spiritual imagination.

- **John of the Cross** – Christian mystic famous for describing the "dark night of the soul."

- **Judaism** – A monotheistic religion centered on covenant, law, and the Hebrew scriptures.

- **Kabbalah** – Jewish mystical tradition exploring divine structure and the soul's journey.

- **Kabbalistic thought** – Teachings on divine emanation, mystical union, and sacred symbolism.

- **Kabbalistic Tree of Life** – Symbolic diagram of divine attributes and paths of creation.

- **Koans** – Zen riddles or paradoxes used to break logical thinking and awaken insight.

- **Kriya Yoga** – A yogic practice using breath and meditation for spiritual awakening.

- **Kundalini** – Dormant spiritual energy said to rise through chakras during awakening.

- **Mandala** – A sacred geometric design symbolizing the cosmos and inner spiritual journey.

- **Mantra** – A sacred sound or phrase repeated for focus, healing, or divine connection.

- **Marsilio Ficino** – Renaissance thinker who revived Neoplatonism and translated Hermetic texts.

- **Martin Luther** – Reformer who challenged Catholic doctrine and sparked the Protestant Reformation.

- **Materialism** – Belief that physical matter is the only or primary reality.

- **Meister Eckhart** – a Christian mystic who emphasized union with God through inner detachment.

- **Metaphor** – A symbolic expression that conveys spiritual truths beyond literal meaning.

- **Moksha** – Liberation from the cycle of birth and rebirth in Hindu and Jain philosophy.

- **Nadi Shodhana** – Yogic breathing technique for purifying energy channels and balancing the mind.

- **Neoplatonism** – Philosophical system blending Plato's ideas with mystical cosmology and ascent.

- **Nirvana** – The ultimate goal in Buddhism: release from suffering and rebirth.

- **Occult** – Hidden or esoteric knowledge involving spiritual forces beyond ordinary perception.

- **Orthodox** – Adhering to established or traditional beliefs, especially in religion.

- **Paracelsus** – Renaissance physician and mystic who integrated alchemy with medicine.

- **Paramahansa Yogananda** – Indian yogi who popularized meditation and Kriya Yoga in the West.

- **Pico della Mirandola** – Renaissance humanist known for his synthesis of mystical traditions.

- **Pranayama** – Yogic breath control practices for energy regulation and mental clarity.

- **Protestant Reformation** – 16th-century movement challenging Catholic authority and promoting direct faith.

- **Pseudoscience** – Beliefs presented as scientific but lacking empirical support or methodology.

- **Ramana Maharshi** – an Indian sage who taught self-inquiry as the path to realization.

- **Rigveda** – Ancient Vedic scripture containing hymns and spiritual philosophy.

- **Rumi** – Persian Sufi poet whose verses celebrate divine love and unity.

- **Samadhi** – A state of meditative absorption or spiritual transcendence in yoga.

- **Samsara** – The cycle of birth, death, and rebirth in Indian religions.

- **Satori** – Sudden enlightenment or awakening in Zen Buddhism.

- **Scholasticism** – Medieval method of learning combining logic, theology, and classical philosophy.

- **Sefirot** – Ten divine attributes in Kabbalah that express God's creative power.

- **Shamanic Trance** – An altered state used by shamans to journey spiritually or heal.

- **Shamanism** – Ancient spiritual practice involving healing, spirits, and altered consciousness.

- **Sheikh** – Spiritual leader or elder in Islamic Sufism.

- **Sufi poets** – Mystics who express divine love through evocative poetry and symbolism.

- **Sufism** – Islamic mysticism focused on inner purification and union with God.

- **Syncretism** – The blending of different religious or spiritual beliefs into a new system.

- **Tantra** – Esoteric path using rituals, energy, and symbols to reach enlightenment.

- **Teresa of Ávila** – Catholic mystic who wrote on prayer and inner spiritual ascent.

- **Third Eye** – Symbol of inner vision, intuition, and higher consciousness.

- **Thomas Aquinas** – Theologian who harmonized Christian faith with Aristotelian philosophy.

- **Tikkun Olam** – Jewish concept of healing and repairing the world through moral action.

- **Torah** – The foundational Jewish text containing law, teachings, and guidance.

- **Upanishads** – Philosophical Hindu texts exploring the nature of reality and the soul.

- **Vision quest** – A rite of passage in indigenous traditions involving solitude and insight.

- **Wahdat al-Wujud** – Sufi concept of the oneness of being; all is unified in God.

- **William James's study of religious experiences** – Classic analysis of how humans experience the divine.

- **Yogic Traditions** – Diverse systems of physical, mental, and spiritual practices in India.

- **Zazen** – Seated meditation at the heart of Zen Buddhist practice.

- **Zen monk** – A practitioner devoted to meditation, mindfulness, and spiritual discipline.

- **Zohar** – Foundational Kabbalistic text exploring mystical aspects of the Torah.

References

- Brett. (2024, July 1). The Mystic Archetype: Characteristics & Challenges – Brett Larkin Yoga. *Brett Larkin Yoga.* https://www.brettlarkin.com/the-mystic-archetype-characteristics-challenges/

- Colombia, R. (2022, March 11). *Indigenous mysticism and its relationship with the environment.* Pressenza. https://www.pressenza.com/2022/03/indigenous-mysticism-and-its-relationship-with-the-environment/

- *Japanese Zen Buddhist Philosophy (Stanford Encyclopedia of Philosophy).* (2024, March 7). https://plato.stanford.edu/entries/japanese-zen/

- Martinuzzi, C. (2020). Mysticism in the Renaissance. In *Springer eBooks* (pp. 1–4). https://doi.org/10.1007/978-3-319-02848-4_1027-1

- Merkur, & Dan. (2025, May 12). *Mysticism | Definition, History, Examples, & Facts.* Encyclopedia Britannica. https://www.britannica.com/topic/mysticism

- *Mysticism (Stanford Encyclopedia of Philosophy).* (2022, June 29). https://plato.stanford.edu/entries/mysticism/

- Waxman, R., PhD. (n.d.). *Correspondences in Jewish*

Mysticism/Kabbalah and Hindu Mysticism/Vedanta-Advaita. https://philarchive.org/rec/WAXCIJ

- Wikipedia contributors. (2025a, May 21). *List of occult symbols.* Wikipedia. https://en.wikipedia.org/wiki/List_of_occult_symbols

- Wikipedia contributors. (2025b, May 25). *Christian mysticism.* Wikipedia. https://en.wikipedia.org/wiki/Christian_mysticism

- Wikipedia contributors. (2025c, May 25). *The varieties of religious experience.* Wikipedia. https://en.wikipedia.org/wiki/The_Varieties_of_Religious_Experience

- Yogitim. (2024, August 20). *The 7 Stages of Kundalini Awakening • Yoga Basics • Yoga Basics.* Yoga Basics. https://www.yogabasics.com/connect/yoga-blog/the-7-stages-of-kundalini-awakening/

- *Austin, D. (2025, May 13). How changing the way you breathe can improve your brain and body. Health. https://www.nationalgeographic.com/health/article/health-benefits-of-breathing-exercises*

- *Cristofori, I., Bulbulia, J., Shaver, J. H., Wilson, M., Krueger, F., & Grafman, J. (2015). Neural correlates of mystical experience. Neuropsychologia, 80, 212–220. https://doi.org/10.1016/j.neuropsychologia.2015.11.021*

- *Harvard Health. (2024, January 31). Mindfulness can help you tame fears and worries. https://www.health.harvard.edu/mind-and-mood/mindfulness-can-help-you-tame-fears-and-worries#:~:text=Sit%20somewhere%20quiet%20and%20close,your%20intrusive%20thoughts%20as%20clouds*

- *Münsterberg, H. (2022, May 25). Psychology and mysticism. The Atlantic. https://www.theatlantic.com/magazine/archive/1899/01/psycholog y-and-mysticism/636988/*

- *Nangle, J. (2025, May 21). Visualization for Spiritual Growth: Making a Spiritual Vision Board -. Jeanne Nangle Soul Coach. https://jeannenangle.com/visualization-for-spiritual-growth-maki ng-a-spiritual-vision-board*

- *O'Sullivan, M. (2025, June 2). Sleeping with the Seasons: How to Sleep Well in Summer According to Chinese Medicine — Escapada Health. Escapada Health. https://www.escapadahealth.com/en/blog/integrated-rituals-into- modern-life*

- *Staff, M. (2025, May 27). How to meditate. Mindful. https://www.mindful.org/how-to-meditate/*

- *Synchronicity: an Acausal connecting Principle – International Association of Analytical Psychology – IAAP. (n.d.). https://iaap.org/jung-analytical-psychology/short-articles-on-analy tical-psychology/synchronicity-an-acausal-connecting-principle/*

- *Tech, Q. C.-. Q. &. E. (2023, September 12). Quantum Mechanics meets Spirituality: Exploring the mystical connection. Medium. https://medium.com/coinmonks/quantum-mechanics-meets-spiritu ality-exploring-the-mystical-connection-427c37f16add*

- *The power of a spiritual community. (n.d.). https://www.kabbalah.com/en/articles/the-power-of-a-spiritual-co mmunity/*

- *Wikipedia contributors. (2025, April 11). Quantum mysticism. Wikipedia. https://en.wikipedia.org/wiki/Quantum_mysticism*

- *Wonder, A. (2024, November 16). Facing Fear: How Embracing*

Mysticism Changed My Relationship with Uncertainty. Medium. https://medium.com/@wonderalice039/facing-fear-how-embracin g-mysticism-changed-my-relationship-with-uncertainty-3cf5a1c16 909

- *6 Powerful benefits of Silent Retreats | Healing Holidays. (n.d.). H e a l i n g H o l i d a y s . https://www.healingholidays.com/blog/6-powerful-benefits-of-silen t-retreats*

- *Felman, A. (2024, March 22). What is mental health? https://www.medicalnewstoday.com/articles/325061*

- *Hazelwood, J. (2023, July 3). Compassion as an act of spiritual growth — James Hazelwood. James Hazelwood. https://www.jameshazelwood.net/blog/2023/7/3/compassion-as-an- act-of-spiritual-growth*

- *Japanese Zen Buddhist Philosophy (Stanford Encyclopedia of Philosophy). (2024, March 7). https://plato.stanford.edu/entries/japanese-zen/*

- *Lee, J. (2024a, October 3). Jungian Alchemy: the secret of inner transformation. This Jungian Life. https://thisjungianlife.com/jungian-alchemy-the-secret-of-inner-tr ansformation/*

- *Lee, J. (2024b, November 21). ECSTATIC TRANSFORMATION: activating the archetype of radical joy. This Jungian Life. https://thisjungianlife.com/ecstatic-transformation/#:~:text=Mysti cal%20traditions%20frame%20ecstasy%20as,sacred%2C%20wher e%20dualities%20are%20transcended*

- *Marie, N., Lafon, Y., Bicego, A., Grégoire, C., Rousseaux, F., Bioy, A., Vanhaudenhuyse, A., & Gosseries, O. (2024). Scoping review on* shamanistic trances practices. *BMC Complementary Medicine and Therapies, 24(1).* https://doi.org/10.1186/s12906-024-04678-w

- *Spirituality & Ethics | Spiritual Heritage Education Network Inc. (n.d.).* https://www.spiritualeducation.org/library/articles/shiv_spirituality_ethics

- *Wikipedia contributors. (2025, June 3). Advaita vedanta. Wikipedia.* https://en.wikipedia.org/wiki/Advaita_Vedanta

- *Astrological Mastery: Unraveling the secrets of the cosmos for personal and professional enlightenment. (n.d.).* https://omniscience.tech/book/al-mastery-secrets-cosmos-enlightenment

- *Epperly, B. (2023, October 17). Mysticism and Social Action: The Spirituality of Howard Thurman. ProgressiveChristianity.org.* https://progressivechristianity.org/resource/mysticism-and-social-action-the-spirituality-of-howard-thurman/

- *Haymond, B. (2019, May 14). Does Mysticism need Community? If so, what kind? Thy Mind, O Human.* https://www.thymindoman.com/does-mysticism-need-community-if-so-what-kind/

- *Houston, B. W. F., Jr. (2024, November 21). Faith in the Modern World: Navigating belief in a digital age. Medium.* https://medium.com/@bishopwfhoustonjr/faith-in-the-modern-world-navigating-belief-in-a-digital-age-0554e41daffd#:~:text=Technology%20as%20a%20Tool%20for,the%20comfort%20of%20their%20homes

- *Magical, mystical and medicinal. (2020, September 25). Europeana.* https://metis-preview-portal.eanadev.org/en/exhibitions/magical-

mystical-and-medicinal

- *Clinic, C. (2022, June 21). The G.L.A.D. technique. The Corvallis Clinic. https://www.corvallisclinic.com/glad-technique/*

www.ingramcontent.com/pod-product-compliance
Lightning Source LLC
Chambersburg PA
CBHW070333130626
46556CB00007B/2842